W9-BCG-562

Prize-Winning Science Fair Projects for Curious Kids

Prize-Winning Science Fair Projects for Curious Kids

Joe Rhatigan & Rain Newcomb

LARK
BOOKS

A Division of
Sterling Publishing Co., Inc.
New York

The Library of Congress has cataloged the hardcover edition as follows:

Rhatigan, Joe.
  Prize-winning science fair projects for curious kids / by Joe Rhatigan & Rain Newcomb.
     p. cm.
  Includes index.
  ISBN 1-57990-478-5
  1. Science projects—Juvenile literature. [1. Science—Experiments—Methodology. 2. Experiments—Methodology. 3. Science projects—Methodology.] I. Newcomb, Rain. II. Title.
Q182.3.R49 2004
507'.8—dc22
                              2003024957

10 9 8 7 6 5 4 3 2 1

Published by Lark Books, a division of
Sterling Publishing Co., Inc.
387 Park Avenue South, New York, NY 10016

First Paperback Edition 2005
© 2004, Lark Books

Distributed in Canada by Sterling Publishing,
c/o Canadian Manda Group, 165 Dufferin Street
Toronto, Ontario, Canada M6K 3H6

Distributed in the U.K. by Guild of Master Craftsman Publications Ltd.,
Castle Place, 166 High Street, Lewes, East Sussex, England BN7 1XU
Tel: (+ 44) 1273 477374, Fax: (+ 44) 1273 478606,
Email: pubs@thegmcgroup.com, Web: www.gmcpublications.com

Distributed in Australia by Capricorn Link (Australia) Pty Ltd.,
P.O. Box 704, Windsor, NSW 2756 Australia

If you have questions or comments about this book, please contact:
Lark Books
67 Broadway
Asheville, NC 28801
(828) 253-0467

Manufactured in China

ISBN 1-57990-478-5 (hardcover) 1-57990-750-4 (paperback)

For information about custom editions, special sales, premium and corporate purchases, please contact Sterling Special Sales Department at 800-805-5489 or specialsales@sterlingpub.com.

Art Director:
CELIA NARANJO
Photographer:
STEVE MANN
Illustrator:
ORRIN LUNDGREN
Cover Designer:
BARBARA ZARETSKY
Associate Art Director:
SHANNON YOKELEY
Editorial Assistance:
DELORES GOSNELL
Technical Consultant:
ELIZABETH SNOKE
Project Consultants:
HOPE BUTTITA &
ELIZABETH SNOKE
Proofreader:
VAL ANDERSON

Contents

INTRODUCTION

Tick, tick, tick, tick, tick, tick, tick, tick, tick, tick….

That's the sound of time ticking away.

Time that's wasting as you sit in your room frantically worrying about your **SCIENCE FAIR PROJECT DEADLINE.**

Brrrinnnggggg! Brrringg!

Yes, it's science fair time again, and this year you've promised not to wait until the very night before the fair to do your experiment. You've even promised yourself to choose an exciting topic that you'll be interested in. Your only problem is you don't know how to deliver on all those promises. Quite frankly, you're stuck.

Well, we've been in the same position as you, although not in the same room, and we've decided to write a book just for people like you who need help getting from "worried kid trying to think of an experiment" to "confident kid impressing a bunch of judges in front of his science fair display."

How useful is this book? Here's an example of just some of the great information this book has to offer:

Things You Don't Need to Do a Good Science Fair Project

- Lab coat
- Lab
- Bunch of tiny white mice
- 400-pound textbook
- Storeroom full of beakers
- Crazy assistant with maniacal laugh

See, wasn't that useful?

How about this tidbit of information:

Things You Absolutely Need in Order to Do a Good and Fun Science Fair Project:

- Your curiosity about the world around you

You're pretty glad you're reading this book now, aren't you?

If you want more, well, that's what we're here for. We've included a chapter on absolutely everything you need, from picking an interesting topic and making a schedule, to doing the experiment and following it through to its successful conclusion. And that's not all. We've also collected 50 amazing projects that are set up so that if you used one of them, you wouldn't be cheating because it will still be up to you to do the work and figure out the results. Or you can use any one of these projects for inspiration to get you started on your own.

Come on, time's ticking away. Let's get started.

Any resemblance to a real mad scientist is purely coincidental!

The Official All-You-Need-to-Know-to-Do-a-Great-Science-Fair-Project Section

You can read all the books on soccer in the world, but that won't make you a great soccer player. You have to actually get your hands (well, your feet) on a soccer ball; go to the park; and kick, dribble, fake out an opponent or two, and every once in a while (this is soccer, after all) score. You figure things out by DOING. Science works the same way. Sure, you learn a lot in class reading textbooks and doing homework, but there's nothing quite like getting your hands dirty doing some science. That's where science fairs come in. Most science fairs ask their participants to DO some real, live science. And then, you get to show off what you learned.

Sometimes science fair projects are judged, and the top winners may get prizes. They may even be invited to higher competitions. And although winning stuff is cool, we're here to say that if you put some effort into doing your own project and work hard at it, you'll probably feel pretty good about yourself and the whole science fair experience, regardless of whether or not you come away with a blue ribbon.

The Secret to Science Fair Success

Behind each successful science fair project is a simple rule: follow the scientific method. As a science fair participant, you'll be asked to research a question, form an opinion as to what the answer to that question is, and then design an experiment to either prove or disprove your opinion. That, in a nutshell, is the scientific method—a step-by-step process that helps you form **and** answer a question.

Scientists spend a lot of time observing, experimenting, guessing, and creatively finding answers to the world's mysteries. The scientific method is one important way scientists look for answers, and it's your ticket to doing well at the next science fair.

Don't worry if you don't totally understand this scientific method thing yet. There's more to come.

Your Plan of Action

Even before getting all involved in doing experiments, testing hypotheses, and becoming the super scientist you always knew you could be, you need a **plan**. A good plan that breaks down your science fair project into totally doable little pieces will make your life a whole lot easier and your project a whole lot more enjoyable.

Step 1: Buy a notebook.

Easy stuff. A no brainer. Proclaim this notebook as your OFFICIAL SCIENCE FAIR PROJECT LOG, and use it only for that purpose.

In this notebook, you'll:

- Keep all your notes, thoughts, and ideas
- Write down the titles and authors of all the books and articles you've read while researching your topic

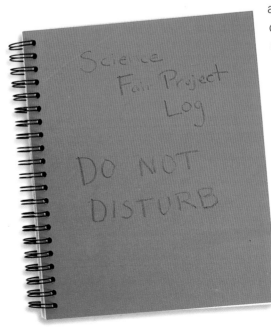

- Develop your hypothesis
- Design your experiment
- Record your data and observations
- Turn your raw data into results
- Write a draft of your written report

Every time you enter information in your log, note the date, time, and anything else you consider important. Is this notebook vital to your project? You bet. Your teacher will most likely want to see your work on your project from beginning to end, and also to make sure you didn't dust off your older sister's project from two years ago. Does this notebook have to be super neat? No. It's mainly for your own use.

Step 2: Write down questions you have.

This is another easy one. Don't assume everyone except you knows all the answers. Write down the questions you have and ask them. Even if you feel they are stupid questions, go ahead and ask. Odds are other students had the same questions but are afraid to ask.

Step 3: Create a schedule you can stick to.

Get a calendar. Mark off today's date and the date your project is due. Count the number of weeks you have to do your science fair project. Spread the different tasks out over the whole time period. Don't wait until the last month, week, or day (!) to try to get everything done. It won't work.

Step 4: Understand the scientific method.

To go any further in this process you have to have a pretty good handle on the scientific method. There are five steps.

1. Ask a question.

2. Research the topic you're asking a question about.

3. Form a personal opinion of what you think the answer will be. This is called a *hypothesis*. It's not a wild guess, especially since you've researched the problem already, but, instead, more of an educated guess.

4. Test your hypothesis by performing an experiment.

5. Draw conclusions after examining your data from the experiment. Did your hypothesis hold up after analyzing your data? What happened?

Checklist for Success #1:

Eight-Week Schedule Checklist

If you have eight weeks before the science fair, you can use this schedule as is. Check off each task as you complete it. Go ahead—it feels good—and it gives you a sense of real accomplishment. Write the dates in the spaces provided, and get to work. If you have more than eight weeks, don't wait. Simply give yourself more time to do some of the tasks. Or, get started and finish early. Hey, why not!?

Week #1 (dates: _____)

- ☐ Choose your topic.
- ☐ Organize your notebook.
- ☐ Ask questions.

Week #2 (dates: _____)

- ☐ Research your chosen topic.

Week #3 (dates: _____)

- ☐ Finish your research.
- ☐ Define your problem.
- ☐ Develop your hypothesis.
- ☐ Design your experiment.

Week #4 (dates: _____)

- ☐ Turn in an experiment summary to your teacher.

- ☐ Gather all needed materials for your experiment.
- ☐ Start your experiment.

Week #5 (dates: _____)

- ☐ Set up an outline for your project report.
- ☐ Continue your experiment.
- ☐ Begin collecting materials for your display.

Week #6 (dates: _____)

- ☐ Continue your experiment.
- ☐ Write the first draft of your project report.
- ☐ Sketch some designs for your display.

Week #7 (dates: _____)

- ☐ Finish your experiment.
- ☐ Revise list of materials needed for the experiment and the steps of the procedure, if necessary.
- ☐ Analyze your data, and draw your conclusions.
- ☐ Revise the project report.

Week #8 (dates: _____)

- ☐ Complete your display.
- ☐ Edit and type the final draft of the project report.
- ☐ Prepare for the fair.

The Fair (date: _____)

The Scientific Method at Work in Your Life

You're walking around your neighborhood one day, and you notice some guy changing the oil in his car. You watch him as he dumps the old oil onto the grass between his and a neighbor's house. Your first reaction is to think, "What a slob!" But wait, a question forms in your mind: "What's going to happen to the grass he just poured all that oil on top of?" You just STATED A QUESTION. Next, you keep walking and recall something your science teacher said about oil pollution. You go home and find your notes. You just GATHERED BACKGROUND INFORMATION. After reading your notes, you decide that oil will affect the growth of the grass. There's your HYPOTHESIS. You have a sneaking suspicion that the oil will kill the grass. This is your PREDICTION. To see whether or not you're right, you walk down the block every day where the guy spilled the oil. You're in the process of TESTING YOUR HYPOTHESIS. Finally, after about three days, you notice that the grass where the oil was spilled has turned yellow and

brown. "Aha," you say. "Just as I thought, oil will kill grass." You've just DRAWN A CONCLUSION. Tah-da! A scientist is born!

When you're trying to decide if you've got a *hypothesis* or a *prediction*, keep this in mind:

- A *hypothesis* states that two things are related.

- A *prediction* guesses how those two things are related.

Step 5: Choose a topic.

Okay, take a deep breath. This one isn't as difficult as it sounds—even if many kids can get stuck on this step for a while. If a topic doesn't immediately come to mind, don't give up. I bet 99.9% of kids don't have a topic the instant the science fair is announced in class.

Checklist for Success #2:
Choosing a Good Topic

- ☐ I'm interested in my topic and am looking forward to learning more about it.

- ☐ I've researched the topic, interviewed professionals, and read extensively about it.

- ☐ My topic can be narrowed down to a question that can be answered by conducting an experiment.

- ☐ My question is open-ended.

- ☐ I can do most of the work myself in the time allotted.

- ☐ My topic follows all rules and guidelines and won't blow up the kitchen.

- ☐ I have teacher approval.

- ☐ I can get all the materials needed for the experiment. (I don't need radioactive space debris or an electron microscope.)

Here are some tips:

● Choose a topic that interests you or that you're curious about, and don't feel you have to choose something scientific that will please teachers, parents, and judges. Ask yourself these questions:

  – What interests me?

  – What do I like to do?

  – Is there something I've always wanted to know the answer to?

● Don't try to send a probe to Mars. Choose a topic that you can do in the time you have. It's perfectly okay (in fact, preferable) to work on something that's not too complicated.

● Live your life as always, but pay closer attention to your surroundings. If you watch television, watch the commercials. Are they telling the truth? Got garbage? Where does all our garbage go, and how much of it is there?

● Read newspapers, magazines, science journals, textbooks, and science fair books. Go to the library.

● Ask any of your teachers (not just your science teacher) for advice and ideas.

● Explore what your parents, friend's parents, family, and neighbors do for a living.

● Visit museums.

● Write down all your ideas in your notebook. Narrow down possible topics until you have one you like best. If you don't have an awesome question yet, that's okay. Doing some research may help.

Step 6: Fine-tune your topic.

This is where you turn your topic into a question that can be answered. Sometimes you may not be able to fine-tune your topic until after you do some research (see step 7 on page 13). So if you have to switch these two steps around, go for it. Here are some tips:

● Make sure your question is not too general, making it impossible to do research and perform an experiment in the time you have.

● Don't ask a question that will be too difficult to answer.

● Make sure the question is open-ended. That means you should not be able to answer it by simply stating "yes" or "no."

DANGER!

Before moving ahead with your project, make sure your science fair project won't be breaking any rules. For example, you can't use dangerous materials, harmful bacteria, ionized radiation, high voltage/amperage electrical equipment, or improperly shielded electrical equipment in your projects. You also can't do an experiment with animals that involves the animals' discomfort, pain, or death. Even if you want to do an experiment on an animal that won't hurt it, ask first.

These two lists will help you focus as you start your research.

● In addition to going to the library, also check out reputable science sites on the Internet, and contact scientists and other professionals to help you with your research. (More on page 15.)

● Make sure your question won't lead to an experiment that will break any science fair rules or regulations. See the box on the left.

Step 7: Research your topic.

Researching means finding as much information on your topic as possible. This ensures that not only will you understand your topic, but you'll also be able to develop a question that will work for your project. The more you understand about your topic at this stage, the easier the rest of the steps will be. Here are some research tips:

● Write down everything you already know about your topic in your notebook. On the next page, write down all the questions you have and what you'd like to learn.

Turning Your Topic Into a Question

You just watched your mom throw some salt into the boiling water that's going to be used to cook tonight's pasta. Whoa! Suddenly you have a great idea for a science fair project. You're going to find out why your mom just did that. Here are a bunch of different questions and why they do and don't work as science fair questions.

"WHY IS SALT USED IN COOKING?"

What works: You're asking about something you're interested in.

What doesn't: It's too general. There's no one experiment you can design to test this question out.

What can you do?: Fine-tune your question by being more specific.

"HEY, MOM, WHY ARE YOU PUTTING SALT IN THE WATER FOR TONIGHT'S PASTA?"

What works: The question is open-ended, and it's getting closer to the question you can ask for your science fair project.

What doesn't: Your mom won't be at the science fair to help you, and she may not have the answer.

What you can do: Make the question more scientific sounding.

"DOES SALT AFFECT THE BOILING POINT OF WATER?"

What works: You're getting closer.

What doesn't: This is a simple yes/no question.

What you can do: Turn the question into an open-ended one.

"HOW DOES SALT AFFECT THE BOILING POINT OF WATER?"

What works: It's simple, to the point, and it's a question that can be answered by doing an experiment.

Section off several pages of your notebook to organize all the information you've collected. Write down names, sources, pages, titles, website addresses, and a summary of each article and chapter you read. Check with your teacher for advice on keeping a bibliography.

Step 8: Develop your hypothesis.

Remember that the hypothesis is your educated guess about the solution to your question or problem. The experiment you design in step 9 will either support or disprove your hypothesis. Going back to the salt in the pasta water example, you might come to the conclusion based on your research and what you witnessed that adding salt to boiling water will cause the water to boil at a higher temperature. Use "I" to state your hypothesis.

"I believe that adding salt to boiling water will affect the boiling temperature of the water."

Step 9: Design your experiment.

It's time to test your hypothesis by putting together a simple experiment. The most important thing to do during this step is to control your *variables*. Variables are anything that can affect the outcome of the experiment. The *independent* (or *experimental*) *variable* is the one thing that the experimenter changes on purpose to see what happens. The *dependent* (or *measured*)

variable is what happens as a result of the change. The variables that are not changed are the *controlled variables* or *controls*. Confused? Here's an example:

You're ready to design your salt-in-the-boiling-water experiment, and you decide that the best way to test your hypothesis is to get a large pot, fill it with water, and boil the water. The amount of water in the pot, what burner you put the pot on, the temperature you set the burner to, and the amount of time it takes the water to boil are all your controls. (In order to have them really be controls, you'll need to measure the amount of water you put in the pot and use the same amount for each test, use the same burner for each test,

and set the burner to the same temperature for each test.) Your independent variable is the amount of salt you add to the boiling water in each test. For your first test, you'll bring the water in the pot to boil without adding any salt and take the temperature of the water. For your second test, dump out the pot, wash and dry it, add the amount of water and salt, bring the water to a boil, and take the temperature of the water again. Do this for each successive test. The temperature readings you record are your dependent variables. The difference in temperatures after each addition of salt (if any) will either support your hypothesis or not.

When designing an experiment, you have to make sure you only have one independent variable. For instance, if you added salt to boiling water and also turned on a fan to blow on the water, you now have two different possible reasons why the water stopped boiling for a moment. Get rid of the fan.

Step 10: Conduct your experiment.

After you've figured out how to do your experiment, it's time to go for it. Gather all the materials you need for the experiment, and follow your steps. Record all your data in your notebook, and take notes on your materials, measurements, observations, and thoughts. Take pictures or draw diagrams of your experiment. And remember that just because something happens once, that doesn't necessarily support your hypothesis. Repeat your experiment. Then, repeat it again. So, in the boiling water experiment, after you've finished your experiment, carefully dump the hot, salty water; wash and dry the pot; and start all over again.

Step 11: Analyze the data and draw conclusions.

After you've collected all your data and you feel confident you have enough, do any calculations that'll help you draw a conclusion. Put together charts or graphs to help you (see page 20 for more on charts and graphs). Then, the big question we've all been waiting for: do your results support your hypothesis?

Your project conclusion is a short summary of your

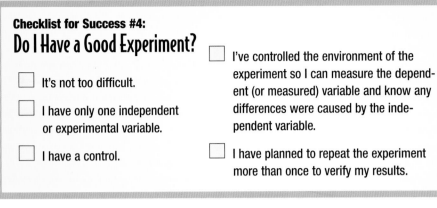

experiment's results and how they relate to your hypothesis. You can also add questions that came up as a result of your experiment.

"As I stated in my hypothesis, I believe salt will affect the boiling temperature of water. My experiment supports my hypothesis. After repeating the experiment three times, the water temperature at its boiling point was higher each time I added salt. If I were to improve this experiment, I would try using sugar instead of salt during a fourth run to see how a different substance affects water."

If your experiment doesn't support your hypothesis, don't worry. It may actually end up being a more interesting situation. Judges won't penalize you if your experiment doesn't support your hypothesis, and they'll be quite impressed if you've thought of possibilities as to why your hypothesis wasn't supported by the experiment.

Step 12: Write the project report.

The project report is the written record of your project. Use your notes to help you record what happened during your experiment, and include:

- A title page that lists the name of the project, your name, grade, and school

- A table of contents that lists what's in the report and what page everything's on

- An *abstract*, which is a brief, one-paragraph overview of the project that includes the title and a summary of the purpose or problem, your hypothesis, and conclusion

- An introduction that states your purpose along with any information that led you to choose this topic

- The list of materials and equipment needed for the experiment

- A paragraph-by-paragraph description of the experiment's procedures, including all variables and how you measured and recorded what happened

- All your data, along with charts and graphs

- Your conclusion

- A list of your sources, along with an acknowledgments page of people who helped you and how they helped you

By the Way...

Interested in trying out the boiling water and salt experiment? Go ahead, but don't rely on our numbers. Also, does throwing salt in boiling water really help pasta cook faster? Some people say, "yes." Others disagree. There's only one way to find out…. And when you're done with your pasta-cooking experiment, don't forget to invite us over for the giant pasta feast.

Checklist for Success #5:
Writing a Good Report

- [ ] I included a title page that lists the name of the project, my name, grade, and school.

- [ ] I devised a table of contents that lists what's in the report and what page everything's on.

- [ ] I included an abstract, which is a brief, one-paragraph overview of the project. The abstract includes the title and a summary of the purpose, hypothesis, and conclusion.

- [ ] My introduction states my purpose along with any information that led me to choose this topic.

- [ ] The list of materials and equipment needed for the experiment is included.

- [ ] The description of my experiment's procedures, including all variables and how I measured and recorded what happened, is included.

- [ ] All of my data is included, along with all charts and graphs with short written summaries for each one.

- [ ] I have a conclusion that tells how I interpreted my results.

- [ ] My sources, including all written materials, as well as anyone I may have interviewed, are listed.

- [ ] I have an acknowledgments page, stating who helped me and how they helped.

Step 13: Put together your display.

For the actual science fair you'll need a display, which is a self-standing, three-paneled piece of cardboard that usually measures 48 x 36 inches [1.2 x .9 m]. Check the rules of your science fair for display size—sometimes a display that's too large can get you disqualified! Display boards can be found at office supply stores. All of your information will be displayed on this board, including your:

✔ Title

✔ Problem/Question

✔ Hypothesis

✔ Abstract

✔ Experimental Materials

✔ Procedure

✔ Data Results

✔ Conclusion

Other tips:

● Use a word-processing program on your computer and a color printer. See if your school's library will let you use one if you don't have a computer at home.

● Make the title big enough to see from a distance. Use stencils if you can't get to a computer.

● Display photographs of the procedure and results.

● Create attractive graphs and tables to show your data.

● Create attractive borders around your pages on the display by gluing the square piece of white paper with the information on it to a slightly bigger piece of colored paper.

● Lay the board on the floor, and arrange the information so it looks good. Get someone to look at it before gluing everything into place. Use rubber cement since most other glues make the paper look crumpled. Don't use staples to attach pages to your display board. The boards aren't thick enough.

● If you used animals (even fish) check the rules before using them, or any part of them, in your display.

Step 14: Enjoy the fair.

At the actual science fair you'll be given space at a table where you'll stand while visitors and judges walk around. And it's your job to tell the whole story of your project to anyone who wants to know. In the space on the table in front of the display, put your written report, notebook, any models made for the experiment, and anything else you can include that represents your experiment. Check your science fair rules to see if there are any items you're not allowed to bring.

If you're part of a judged science fair, the judges may look at all the projects while you're not in the room, and then, later, interview you in front of your project. Most judges use a point system to judge projects, and judging varies from competition to competition. If you've followed all 13 steps up to this point, then all you need to do at the fair is relax and be yourself. You should have no problem answering questions about your project. Don't feel like you have to memorize your project. Have confidence in your work and yourself. Answer questions thoroughly, and don't be afraid to say you don't know an answer to a question. (Tell judges that the question didn't come up in your research!) Judges may ask how you'll continue your project. Mention interesting questions that came up as you worked on the project. Judges are not out there to

Checklist for Success #6:
What the Judges Look For

☐ My project shows original thinking and investigation of an original idea. (You won't get a lot of points for a project that has been done every year for the last 30 years.)

☐ My project is well organized.

☐ I show that I've used the scientific method and have defined my variables and controls.

☐ I did my research and documented it.

☐ I used a notebook to collect data and research.

☐ I worked carefully on the experiment.

☐ I presented my materials to the judges in an organized and knowledgeable way and answered questions accurately.

☐ I used tables, graphs, and illustrations in interpreting data.

☐ I know what I'm talking about, and I understand the science involved in my experiment.

☐ I have a display that's attractive, well labeled, and easily understood.

☐ I have a complete and comprehensive report.

Any resemblance to a real science fair judge is purely coincidental!

"get" you. They simply want to reward students who have worked hard, learned a lot, and done a great job.

And that's about it. Good luck with your project. And remember, being a winner isn't simply about getting an award. It's about being proud of the time and work and sweat you put into your project. And perhaps you're a little bit smarter, a little more curious, and that much closer to being a true explorer of the world around you.

Charts, Graphs, and Tables

Tables and graphs not only look great on your display board, but they also present important information in a way that makes your data easy to understand. Judges can see the information clearly and quickly. There are many different ways you can present your information visually, and below are four popular examples.

DATA TABLES

This simple table is useful for recording and organizing all of your data before creating a more visually appealing chart or graph. When using a table, be sure to label all of your columns and include units of measurement in the headings. The left-hand column usually shows your independent variable, while the columns to the right show your dependent variable. See examples #1 and #2.

Once you've analyzed your data in your table, decide which of the following graphs or charts to use to help visualize your results.

BAR GRAPH

Bar graphs are great for showing comparisons or how something changes. You can use a bar graph to compare water temperature after adding different amounts of salt or to compare how different classes did on a certain test. Label the horizontal axis with the "object" being examined (water with salt added). Label the vertical axis to reflect what is being measured (temperature of the water).

Example #1

TABLE 1. SCIENCE TEST SCORE FOR GRADE 5 CLASSES BROKEN DOWN BY HOW LONG STUDENTS STUDIED

Study Time (min.)	Class 1 (points scored out of 100)	Class 2 (points scored out of 100)	Class 3 (points scored out of 100)	Class 4 (points scored out of 100)	Average Number of Points Scored
0	45	55	35	48	45.75
15	55	57	38	60	52.5
30	73	80	65	81	74.75
45	89	91	83	95	89.5
60	98	100	90	100	97
60 +	100	100	95	100	98.75

Example #2

TABLE 2. TEMPERATURE IN WHICH WATER BOILED WITH DIFFERENT AMOUNTS OF SALT ADDED

Solution	Boiling Point (°F)
Water	212.9
Water + 1 tablespoon salt	215.6
Water + 2 tablespoons salt	218.3
Water + 3 tablespoons salt	221.0

GRAPH 1. BOILING POINT OF WATER/SALT SOLUTIONS

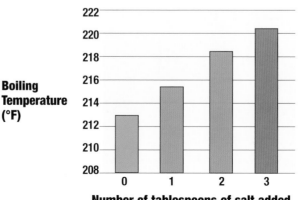

LINE GRAPH

A line graph is great for showing how things change over a period of time, often indicating trends or patterns. You could use a line graph to show the number of students absent over a period of a school year. The horizontal axis shows a period of time (months), while the vertical axis shows the amount of change (number of students absent). What trend do you notice with the following line graph?

GRAPH 2. NUMBER OF STUDENTS IN GRADE 5 CLASSES ABSENT DURING SCHOOL YEAR

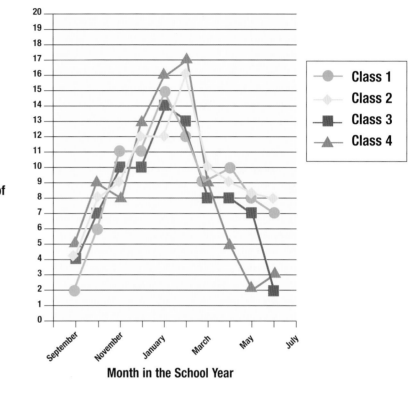

Number of Students Absent

Month in the School Year

PIE CHART

Also referred to as a circle graph, a pie chart presents information in percentages. The whole circle equals 100 percent, and the different pieces of the pie make up different portions of the whole. Pie charts do not show changes over periods of time. For example, you want to find out students' preferences at the lunch line. Your pie chart could look like the chart on the right.

A final note:

When using tables or graphs, make sure to give them titles and number them like the graphs and charts are in these examples. Don't forget to label the axes!

GRAPH 3. STUDENT FOOD CHOICE PERCENTAGES

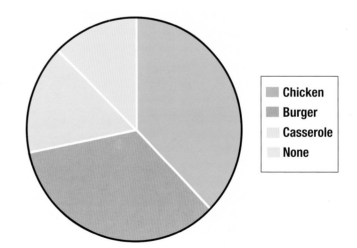

- Chicken
- Burger
- Casserole
- None

The PROJECTS!

The projects in the next three chapters explore three major branches of science: biology, physical science, and chemistry. If the project requires adult supervision or assistance, there will be an ADULT SUPERVISION REQUIRED icon at the top of the project page. Take this seriously. Some experiments require the use of stoves, drills, acids, and chemicals; and even though science is fun, it also pays to be careful.

Each project is broken down into different sections.

The **PROBLEM/PURPOSE** asks the question that the experiment seeks to answer. Please note that there is no section for hypothesis. It's your job to do the research and come up with your own hypothesis.

The **EXPERIMENT SUMMARY** gives you a basic idea of how you'll conduct the experiment.

WHAT YOU NEED is your supply list of everything you'll need to do the experiment. Please note that each list tells you how many volunteers or plant seeds, etc., you'll

need for a valid experiment. Remember, however, that the more trials you perform, the more valid your results will be. So, find more volunteers or use more plants whenever possible.

The **EXPERIMENTAL PROCEDURE** provides step-by-step instructions for doing the experiment.

The **CONCLUSION** gives you questions, advice, and general assistance to help you find your conclusion.

For many of the projects you can **TAKE A CLOSER LOOK** and delve deeper into the topic. Sometimes this section provides more information about the conclusion, and other times it includes facts, tidbits, and other information that can help you with your research.

WHAT ELSE YOU CAN DO shows related ideas and other experiments to try.

Read the whole project before deciding it's the project for you. Use the Take a Closer Look section to help you start your research. Also, make sure you can get all the materials you need. If the What You Need section mentions that you need a bug zapper, make sure you can find one you can use before continuing with the project.

Biology

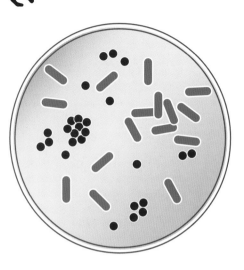

Biology is the science of life, and there's an awful lot of life out there to study. Perhaps that's why kids love to do biology science fair projects. A typical science fair may have up to twice as many biology projects as chemistry or physical science projects. And it's easy to see why: plants are easy to work with, there are always people around to study, animals fascinate us, and bugs are just plain fun. So, if you've ever been curious about seeds, food, dog germs, bacteria, schoolmate behavior, bad drivers, mold, rutabagas, birds, our five senses, farming, and the pitter patter of your heart, then check out this group of projects first.

"Now, repeat after me: Only Teacher is allowed to bring animals to class."

Pooch Smooch

Some people don't mind the sloppy wet affections of their family dog. Meanwhile, there are those who steer clear of those in-your-face kisses. Worried about dog germs? Then, here's an experiment to slobber over.

PROBLEM/PURPOSE

How does the rate of bacterial growth in dog saliva and human saliva compare?

EXPERIMENT SUMMARY

You'll test saliva from a dog and from a human to determine which grows more bacteria in the shortest amount of time.

WHAT YOU NEED

- 6 sterile nutrient agar petri dishes*
- Permanent marker
- Soap and water
- A friendly dog
- Sterile cotton swabs
- Bleach

*Petri dishes are available at science supply stores and in many stores that sell school supplies. (Ask your teacher if you're having trouble finding them.)

EXPERIMENTAL PROCEDURE

1. Label three dishes "human" and three "dog."

2. Make sure neither you or your volunteer dog have eaten or had any treats in the last hour. Using one sterile cotton swab, gently swab the inside of the dog's mouth, collecting some saliva. (You may need to just swab around the gums, depending on how drooly the dog is.)

3. Carefully lift the lid of the first "dog" petri dish, and gently swipe the saliva onto the agar. Be careful not to press down on the agar. Quickly place the lid back on the dish. Discard the cotton swab. Repeat with the other two "dog" dishes, using a new sterile cotton swab for each dish. Wash your hands after each swab.

4. With a new sterile cotton swab, gently swab the inside of your own mouth. Carefully lift the lid of the first "human" petri dish and gently swipe the first "human" dish. Be careful not to press down on the agar. Quickly place the lid back on the dish. Discard the swab. Repeat with the other two "human" petri dishes, using a new sterile cotton swab for each dish.

5. Place the dishes in an area that is at room temperature and where they won't be disturbed.

6. Check the dishes every 24 hours until you see bacterial growth, and write down your observations. Don't open the dishes. Estimate the percentage of dog bacterial growth and human bacterial growth in the dishes. Wash your hands after handling the dishes.

7. Once the experiment is complete, make a bleach solution of 1 part bleach to 10 parts water. Open the petri dishes, being careful not to touch the bacterial growth, and soak them in the bleach solution for 30 minutes. This will kill any harmful bacteria. Throw the dishes away, and wash your hands well.

CONCLUSION

Which group of dishes grew bacteria the quickest—the dog or the human? Draw pictures or take photographs of the dishes to record your observations. How long did it take for growth to appear in each dish? Were more bacteria present in the dog saliva or human saliva? Based on your findings, whose mouth is "cleaner"?

TAKE A CLOSER LOOK

● Germs in the mouths of animals tend to be species-specific, meaning that a dog bite is more dangerous to another dog than to a human. Likewise, a human bite is more dangerous to a human than a dog bite. However, that doesn't mean a human can't get a bacterial infection from a dog bite. If its owners do not properly care for their dog, it can transmit roundworm and rabies to humans and other animals. However, most harmful dog germs are usually harmless to humans. So, chances are, if you know the dog is well taken care of, it's safe to get the licks!

WHAT ELSE YOU CAN DO

● Test your cat's saliva versus your dog's to see which grows bacteria the quickest.

DISPLAY TIPS

● Whatever you do, do not take your bacteria samples to the fair. You'll most likely be disqualified for endangering the health of your peers and the judges. (It is bacteria, after all.) Instead, use the pictures you drew or photographs you took for your display.

Zapped!

Nobody likes mosquitoes, but will using a bug zapper keep you from getting bit?

What kind of bugs do bug zappers actually kill?

EXPERIMENT SUMMARY

You'll collect the dead bugs zapped by a bug zapper one evening, and figure out the ratio of mosquitoes killed versus other bugs killed.

WHAT YOU NEED

► Bug zapper (also known as an electronic insect-control system)
► White paper or poster board
► Rocks
► Container to collect dead bugs
► ½-inch (1.3 cm) paintbrush
► Tweezers
► Insect guide

EXPERIMENTAL PROCEDURE

1. Check the weather report and choose a dry, calm night during the

summer to do your experiment. Since your science fair is probably held in late winter or early spring, you may need to think ahead to do this project.

2. On the evening of your experiment, put the bug zapper in your yard, and cover the ground around the zapper with the white paper or poster board. The paper will collect the falling insects. Anchor the white paper or poster board with rocks. Go to bed and let the zapping begin.

3. The next morning go back outside and collect the dead insects. Carefully brush them into your container with the paintbrush, or use the tweezers to pick them up. Don't forget to brush any insects that landed on the zapper into your container.

4. Find a safe spot to count your insects. Place the white paper over your work surface to make the bugs easier to see. Use the tweezers to separate insects into piles according to what type of insect it is. Use the insect guide to help you identify your insects. Some of the fried insects you'll find may include moths, beetles, flies, bees, ants, dragonflies, and wasps.

5. Record how many of each insect got zapped.

CONCLUSION

Create a pie chart showing the percentage of mosquitoes killed compared to the rest of the insects. Of the insects catalogued, how many are actually considered beneficial? Do your numbers support the use of a bug zapper to rid your yard of biting insects?

TAKE A CLOSER LOOK

• According to manufacturers, bug zappers lure insects (especially mosquitoes) with ultraviolet light, and kill them with electricity.

• Some scientific surveys show that less than ¼ of 1 percent of the bugs killed by bug zappers are biting insects. In fact, not only do bug zappers fail to kill many mosquitoes, they actually tend to kill the non-biting male mosquitoes more than the blood-sucking females. Plus, the electrocuted bug body parts flying everywhere can spread bacteria, especially if you're having a cookout. Yuck!

WHAT ELSE YOU CAN DO

• Most scientists and many nighttime outdoor enthusiasts believe that traditional bug zappers are ineffective against biting insects and do more harm to insects that are good for us. Compare a bug zapper to a newer design—perhaps one that emits *octenol*, a non-toxic, pesticide-free pheromone that supposedly attracts mosquitoes. Or compare a bug zapper to one that emits carbon dioxide. How do the ratios of mosquitoes versus other bugs killed compare?

• Another way to set up this experiment is to test which insects are most attracted to ultraviolet light.

DISPLAY TIPS

• Create a food chain web that shows what animals would have eaten each kind of bug killed in the bug zapper. What would happen if everybody used bug zappers?

Hang Up and Drive?

You've probably seen someone swerving all over the road while talking on a cell phone, or perhaps you've heard that many states have passed laws making it illegal to talk on a cell phone and drive at the same time. Does chatting on a cell phone really make a difference in someone's ability to concentrate and drive?

PROBLEM/PURPOSE

How does being on a cell phone affect motor skills and reaction time?

EXPERIMENT SUMMARY

You'll test your volunteers' ability to talk on the phone and play a video game at the same time.

WHAT YOU NEED

▸ **Car-driving video game**
▸ **Steering wheel game control**
▸ **Several volunteers**
▸ **Cell phone**
▸ **Helper**

EXPERIMENTAL PROCEDURE

1. Choose a video game that none of your volunteers are familiar with. Make sure the video game is a driving game in which you use a steering wheel. (If you are unable to find such a game, at least find a game that can be played more or less with one hand.)

2. Have your first volunteer play the video game five times to get the hang of it.

3. Take a short break, and then have the volunteer play the game five times.

Average the scores of the second five games, and record the average.

4. Give the volunteer the cell phone, then go to another room and call him or her. Stay on the phone until the volunteer has played five more games. Make sure your volunteer is actually talking on the phone and not just saying "Uh-huh."

5. Have a helper record the scores of those five games. Average them.

6. Repeat steps 2 through 5 with the other volunteers.

CONCLUSION

Compare the initial video game scores (when your volunteers weren't on the phone) to the scores when the volunteers were on the phone. How different are they? What can you conclude about how talking on a cell phone affects response time and concentration?

WHAT ELSE YOU CAN DO

● Alternate the times your volunteer plays on the phone and without the phone. This will help you make sure that better scores in the last few games your volunteer plays aren't because he or she has gotten better at the game.

● Test whether a clear-reception call or a staticky call makes a difference in the volunteers' ability to play the video game. Simply talk on the phone clearly for one set of games, and then crumple up some paper by the mouthpiece of the phone for the next set of tests with the same volunteer. What do your results say about the effect of cell phone reception and driver safety?

● Some people say that holding a conversation on a cell phone while driving is the same as talking to a passenger or listening to a CD. Try the same experiment, but then also sit next to your volunteers and talk to them for another five games. Then, have your volunteers try to change a CD in a CD player while playing. How do the average scores compare to the average scores while playing with the cell phone?

DISPLAY TIPS

● If your state has a law against cell phone use while driving, include data the state used to prove the law would be a good one. Compare the state's results with yours.

Horrorscopes

This morning your horoscope said that you were going to have such a horrible day you should just stay in bed. Funny though—you had the best day of your life. Have you wondered how accurate astrology is?

How accurate are the predictions that horoscopes make?

EXPERIMENT SUMMARY

You'll show a group of volunteers the horoscopes from the previous day. They'll pick which horoscope they think is theirs based on what happened to them the day before.

WHAT YOU NEED

▶ 5 or more volunteers (the more the merrier)

▶ Daily horoscope from a local newspaper or Internet source

EXPERIMENTAL PROCEDURE

1. Gather your volunteers. Make copies of the survey on the right, and have each of your volunteers fill one out. If any of your volunteers answer that he or she does read the horoscopes every day, make sure that you don't use the same horoscope that person reads.

2. On the first day of your experiment, photocopy all of the horoscopes from the day before. Leave out the part about what astrological sign it is, and mix up the order that they were printed in. Make a copy for each volunteer.

3. Give the horoscopes to your volunteers, and ask them to pick the one that most accurately describes their day yesterday. Record the results and keep them secret.

4. Repeat steps 2 and 3 for three days.

CONCLUSION

How often did your volunteers choose the right horoscope? How often did they choose the wrong one? Did the volunteers who knew more about horoscopes make better guesses? Turn your data into a bar graph.

TAKE A CLOSER LOOK

● Were there certain horoscopes that people were more or less likely to pick? What were these horoscopes about? Is there a correlation between the subject matter and whether or not a horoscope was picked?

● When you tell your volunteers what their horoscopes actually were at the end of three days, watch how they react.

● Were people of a certain sign more likely to be right than others? Did anyone consistently pick the predictions for one sign? Was it the right sign or not?

The Survey Questions

Name

Birth date

Do you know your astrological sign?

What is it?

How much do you know about your sign (not much, a little, or a lot)?

Do you read your horoscope every day?

If so, which horoscope do you read?

DISPLAY TIPS

● Decorate your display with fun stars, planets, and constellations. You can also include information on the 12 signs of the zodiac.

Take a Closer Look
Astrology, Sham Science

Do you read your horoscope every day? Do you believe that your personality and character can be pinpointed to the date and time of your birth? Do you believe your entire future, including how you'll do on your math test, what your career will be, and who you'll marry, can be figured out by the positions of the moon and planets? If you do, you have fallen for a pseudo science.

What's that?

A pseudo science is a bunch of ideas based on theories that are said to be scientific, when, in fact, they are not. Why is astrology considered a pseudo science? Well, since astrology cannot be backed up by any valid evidence and doesn't hold up against experimentation, it's considered a sham. All lies. A big put on.

But, wait! Back up a moment. Where's your evidence?

Good scientist! Here:

● With the rise of the science of astronomy, scientists have found no proof that planets and stars can influence people. First of all, they are too far away to exert a gravitational force over us. And, second, what exactly is supposed to be shooting forth from these celestial bodies when they're in certain positions that causes us to become doctors instead of lawyers?

● Ask yourself this question: Do you really think $\frac{1}{12}$ of the human population (nearly 550 million people for each sign of the zodiac) will have the same kind of day, every day?

● According to astrology, all the celestial bodies in the sky influence us, and since there are billions of stars in our galaxy alone, how could you possibly create a horoscope that took all those stars and planets into consideration?

● How about the results from the experiment on page 30?

Here are just a few of the pseudo sciences that are out there for you to try and debunk:

● UFOs
● Ghosts and poltergeists
● Fortune-telling
● Tarot cards
● Chiromancy (palm reading)
● ESP (extra sensory perception)
● Crop circles
● Spoon bending
● The Bermuda Triangle
● Dowsing (using a forked stick to find underground water)
● Pyramid power (the belief that pyramids have healing powers)
● Crystal power (see Pyramid power)
● Seances (the belief that we can talk to the dead)

Skin-tilating

What's your largest organ? No, not your lungs, but your skin! An adult's skin can weigh about 8 pounds (3.6 kg). Your skin is sensitive to pressure, touch, and temperature. This experiment tests where on your skin you're most sensitive to touch.

PROBLEM/PURPOSE

What parts of the body are most or least sensitive to touch?

EXPERIMENT SUMMARY

You'll make a Von Frey device using different sizes of fishing line. Then you'll use it to test the touch sensitivity of different parts of people's bodies.

WHAT YOU NEED

▶ **Scissors**

▶ **Ruler**

▶ **5 different diameters of monofilament fishing line**

▶ **Tape**

▶ **5 craft sticks**

▶ **Marker or pen**

▶ **10 volunteers**

EXPERIMENTAL PROCEDURE

1. Cut one 2-inch (5.1 cm) strand from the smallest diameter fishing line. Tape the strand to the first craft stick so that about 1½ inches (3.8 cm) hangs down from the tip of the stick. Use the marker or pen to label the craft stick with the size of the fishing line.

2. Repeat step 1 with the rest of the sizes of fishing line and craft sticks.

3. Make a data table to record your observations. Write the sizes of fishing line across the top of the page. Down the left side, write: index fingertip, cheek, palm, back of hand, forearm, inside forearm, neck, back of neck, elbow, and back of leg. These are your testing spots. Make a copy of the data table for every volunteer.

4. Have each of your volunteers wear a short-sleeved T-shirt and shorts to the testing session. Make sure that you schedule all of your tests on the same day. Humidity can actually affect the size of the fishing line, so a change in the weather could alter your results.

5. Have the first volunteer close his or her eyes and place one hand on a table face-up. Hold the Von Frey device with the smallest fishing line over the volunteer's index finger.

6. Carefully lay the fishing line on the volunteer's fingertip so that the line bends slightly.

7. Ask the volunteer whether he or she felt it, and mark "yes" or "no" on the chart.

8. Repeat steps 5 through 7 with the rest of the body parts.

9. Once you've finished with the body parts, move onto the next sized fishing line, and go through the body parts again. Repeat with all the sizes of fishing line.

10. Repeat steps 5 through 9 with the rest of your volunteers.

CONCLUSION

Once you've completed your experiment and calculated your results, choose a color for each volunteer, and plot their responses on a bar graph. Which body part is the most sensitive? What is least sensitive? Was it consistent for each volunteer? Did gender make a difference? What other factors could have contributed to your results?

TAKE A CLOSER LOOK

● What you're testing in this experiment is the skin's *detection threshold*, which is the smallest amount of touch that someone notices. Your skin has several different types of receptors that trigger a series of nerve impulses. You will only feel the stimulus if the nerve impulses make their way to your brain. Not every part of your body has the same number or same type of receptors. There are less touch receptors on the back and legs. In fact, according to some scientists, your face is almost 500 times more sensitive to touch than your leg. Why do you think we need more touch receptors in some places rather than others?

WHAT ELSE YOU CAN DO

● During the summer months, calculate on what parts of your body you and your family get the most mosquito bites. Are bites concentrated on your hands and face or more on your back and legs? How does this relate to the sensitivity of your skin on different parts of you body?

DISPLAY TIPS

● Bring your Von Frey devices to the fair. Research who Von Frey was and why he developed his first device. Include this information on your display if you want. Demonstrate the devices on the judges.

Who Owns the Road?

Will a person in a sports car drive more recklessly than someone in a mini van? Try this experiment to see whether or not the TYPE of car someone drives affects the WAY that person drives.

PROBLEM/PURPOSE

What's the correlation between car type and a driver's willingness to obey a stop sign?

EXPERIMENT SUMMARY

You'll pick a spot near a stop sign and see what kinds of cars are most likely to either obey or disobey the sign.

WHAT YOU NEED

▶ Paper and pencil
▶ Safe intersection with a stop sign

EXPERIMENTAL PROCEDURE

1. Make a chart to record your observations. Write down different types of cars (mini-van, SUV, etc.) along the top of the chart. On the left side of the chart, write down the way the drivers react to the stop sign (stopped, rolled through, slowed down, etc.)

2. Choose a stop sign to use for your experiment. (Make sure an adult knows where you are, and don't get too close to the traffic.)

3. Start tracking vehicles as they stop or don't stop at the stop sign. Record your observations for two hours.

4. Observe the traffic in the same spot for the same two-hour time span every day for one week. Record your observations.

CONCLUSION

Once you have your raw data, organize it into a series of pie charts, one for each type of car. Are your results conclusive? Does one vehicle or type of vehicle stand out as most likely not to stop at a stop sign?

WHAT ELSE YOU CAN DO

● Do the same experiment, but organize your data according to the color of each vehicle, by the gender or age of the driver, or by the brand of car driven.

Beak Freak!

Instead of a knife and fork, birds eat with their beaks, which can act as chisels, hooks, spears, straws, and hammers. When observing birds, check out their beaks, and see if they match what they're eating.

PROBLEM/PURPOSE

How does the shape of a bird's beak affect diet?

EXPERIMENT SUMMARY

You'll set up plates of food for birds to eat and observe which birds eat from the plates.

WHAT YOU NEED

► **Wild seed mixture**
► **Cheese**
► **Live worms**
► **Fat stripped from meat (wash your hands well after handling meat)**
► **Dried fruit**
► **Bread crumbs**
► **5 or 6 terra-cotta plant saucers**
► **Bird guide**

EXPERIMENTAL PROCEDURE

1. Place each food item in a different terra-cotta plant saucer, and put the plates out in the open, preferably off the ground. A picnic table, large rock, or a wooden bench would work well.

2. Watch to see who eats where. Take notes, and use the bird field guide to figure out which birds are eating what.

3. Experiment with other foods such as sunflower seeds, uncooked oatmeal, and popcorn.

CONCLUSION

Compare the food each type of bird was attracted to with the shape and size of the bird's beak. How did the bird use its beak to get the food? Why don't birds all just eat the same kind of food?

TAKE A CLOSER LOOK

● Seed eaters such as cardinals and sparrows have short, strong, and thick bills for cracking seeds.

● Hawks, owls, and eagles have sharp, curved bills for tearing meat.

● Woodpeckers have strong, long, chisel-like bills for creating holes in trees.

● Hummingbirds have long, straw-like bills that they use to sip nectar from flowers.

● Insect eaters such as warblers and Western Meadowlarks have pointed, thin bills so they can reach into holes when grubbing for food.

● Crows have a multi-purpose bill that allows them to eat just about anything they want, from fruit and seeds to insects and fish.

● Vermilion Flycatchers have a wide bill surrounded by bristles that work to funnel flying insects into its mouth while the bird is in the air.

● Ducks have long, flat bills that strain plants and animals from the water.

● Birds such as herons and kingfishers have spear-like bills for fishing.

Huddling for Heat

Have you ever seen a pile of sleeping puppies? Why do they all want to be the one squashed on the bottom?

PROBLEM/PURPOSE

How does the distance between warm bodies affect their cooling rate?

EXPERIMENT SUMMARY

You'll compare how fast bodies cool when they're alone and when they're huddled together.

WHAT YOU NEED

- ▶ 4 identical glass bottles
- ▶ Water
- ▶ Pot
- ▶ Use of a stovetop
- ▶ Oven mitts
- ▶ Towel
- ▶ 4 thermometers
- ▶ Plastic wrap

EXPERIMENTAL PROCEDURE

1. Heat a pot of water until the water is 150°F (65.5 C°). Completely fill one bottle with the hot water.

2. Quickly dry off the outside of the bottle. Place a thermometer in the opening of the bottle, and seal the top with the plastic wrap.

3. When the temperature on the thermometer stops rising, record this as the initial temperature of the water.

4. Record the temperature every two minutes for 30 minutes. This is your control.

5. Reheat the pot of water until the temperature again reaches 150°F (65.5 C°). Completely fill each of the four bottles with hot water.

6. Quickly dry off the outside of each bottle. Place a thermometer in the opening of each bottle, and seal the tops with the plastic wrap.

7. Place the bottles in a tight square so they are all touching each other.

8. When the temperature on each thermometer stops rising, record this as the initial temperature of the bottles.

9. Record the temperatures of each bottle every two minutes for 30 minutes.

10. Repeat the steps 1 through 6, placing the bottles in a large square so the bottles are about 12 inches from each other. Make sure your initial temperature is the same as the first trial.

CONCLUSION

Make a line graph of temperature versus time for each arrangement of bottles. How did the cooling rate of the huddled bottles compare to the control bottle? How did it compare to the spread out bottles? In which configuration did the "animals" conserve the most heat?

TAKE A CLOSER LOOK

● Animals lose heat through their skin by *radiation* and *convection*. The energy created by the sleeping animal is radiated out of its body as heat. The cool air surrounding the sleeping animal whisks the heat away. More heat rises out of the animal to replace the heat in the air that was lost (convection).

● Huddling allows animals to decrease the amount of skin (or fur or feathers) exposed to the air so they lose less heat.

● Warm-blooded animals, such as mammals and birds, have to keep their bodies within a certain temperature range. If the temperature outside is colder than their bodies, the animals have to generate their own heat by eating. Most of the food that warm-blooded animals eat in the winter is used to keep them warm. Huddling helps preserve the heat in the animal's body. Cold-blooded animals, such as reptiles and fish, don't generate their own heat. They don't need to—their bodies adapt to the temperature.

● Sea otters huddle to stay warm in the cold oceans. Often they will hold hands or tie themselves together with kelp before going to sleep. That way, they won't drift apart in the night.

● Mammals aren't the only creatures who huddle. Some insects do it too. Honeybees crowd together and beat their wings to create heat in the winter. Other insects, such as sowbugs and pillbugs, huddle together to prevent dehydration during the day. This helps keep the water in their bodies that they need to survive from evaporating into the air.

WHAT ELSE YOU CAN DO

● Figure out how many "animals" are needed in order to best benefit from huddling.

DISPLAY TIPS

● Go to a pet store and ask if you can take photographs of their mice, rabbits, and even lizards huddling in their tanks and cages. Use the photographs on your display.

Moldy Slices of Life

Before refrigerators, people had to either eat their food very quickly or find a way to keep their leftovers from getting rotten. One way was to stick the food in a snow bank, but people who couldn't rely on snow to preserve their food used natural preservatives, such as salt and vinegar. Were those methods effective? Here's one way to find out.

PROBLEM/PURPOSE

How do natural preservatives compare to modern refrigeration in the fight against decay, and which natural preservative works best in preserving bread?

EXPERIMENT SUMMARY

You'll use bread with no preservatives as your food sample. Each slice will be dunked in a solution of water and a preservative (except for the refrigerated piece and a control). The slices will be observed for signs of decay.

WHAT YOU NEED

- 9 bowls
- Measuring spoons
- Salt
- Water
- White vinegar
- Lemon juice
- Sugar
- Fresh garlic, minced
- Fresh rosemary, chopped
- Mustard
- 9 slices of bakery-fresh bread (make sure the bread has no preservatives)
- Bread knife (optional)
- 9 small plates
- Marker
- Tape
- Fork
- Use of a refrigerator

EXPERIMENTAL PROCEDURE

1. Look at the chart on the next page, and mix each solution in a separate bowl.

2. If your bread isn't already sliced, slice it in pieces 1 inch (2.5 cm) thick, and select nine slices that are the same size.

3. Write the solution on each of the nine plates with the marker and a piece of tape.

4. Dunk the first slice into bowl #1 for 5 seconds or until it's wet throughout. Remove it carefully with the fork, and place it on the plate that matches that solution.

5. Repeat with the rest of the solutions. Place plate #9 in the refrigerator.

6. Place the other plates in the same dark, warm location (someplace where you won't have to worry about bugs), and leave undisturbed.

7. Create a data table to catalog your observations.

8. Observe the conditions of each slice every day for two weeks.

Bowl 1: 3 teaspoons (15 g) salt, ½ cup (120 mL) water

Bowl 2: 3 teaspoons (15 mL) vinegar, ½ cup (120 mL) water

Bowl 3: 3 teaspoons (15 mL) lemon juice, ½ cup (120 mL) water

Bowl 4: 3 teaspoons (15 g) sugar, ½ cup (120 mL) water

Bowl 5: 3 teaspoons (15 g) minced garlic, ½ cup (120 mL) water

Bowl 6: 3 teaspoons (15 g) rosemary, ½ cup (120 mL) water

Bowl 7: 3 teaspoons (15 mL) mustard, ½ cup (120 mL) water

Bowl 8: ½ cup (120 mL) water

Bowl 9: ½ cup (120 mL) water

Touch them, smell them, and write down what colors they turn. Record the date that each of the bread slices dries out.

TAKE A CLOSER LOOK

Rotting occurs when bacteria such as fungus and viruses begin to eat the food. As they eat, they generate acids that poison the food with toxins to keep other microbes away. Bacteria thrive in warm, humid temperatures, but chemicals such as salt will keep many of them away.

WHAT ELSE YOU CAN DO

Determine what conditions are best for decay by putting the same food item in different locations that have different temperatures. Or, see if light affects decay.

Study the effect vacuum-sealing foods has on decomposition.

DISPLAY TIPS

Since you can't bring your rotten food to the fair, take lots of pictures so that you're carefully documenting your observations.

Gravity Got You Down?

Gravity is pulling us down to the ground every minute of every day. How come plants grow straight up?

How do seedlings react to being turned upside down?

EXPERIMENT SUMMARY

You'll manipulate the position of seedlings to observe the effect gravity has on root and stem growth.

WHAT YOU NEED

▶ **Seed germinator (see page 41)**

▶ **Sunny window**

▶ **Ruler**

▶ **Protractor**

EXPERIMENTAL PROCEDURE

1. Make the seed germinator on the next page. Place the germinator, with seeds, in a sunny window.

2. Observe your seeds at the same time every day. Record any changes you notice. Measure the length of stem and root growth with a ruler.

Measure the direction of stem and root growth with a protractor. Count and measure the number and size of any leaves. You may also wish to sketch a picture of your seeds each day.

3. Once the roots of the seedlings are about

1 inch (2.5 cm) long, carefully remove the CD case from the bottle.

4. Remove half of the seedlings from the paper towels and turn them upside down so the roots are pointing upward. The seeds that are still right-side up are your control.

5. Continue making the same observations you did in step 2.

CONCLUSION

How did the plants react to a change in direction? What patterns did you observe? What surprised you about what happened?

TAKE A CLOSER LOOK

● Seedlings normally grow vertically, with the shoot or stem growing upward and the root growing down. Believe it or not, plants can detect gravity, and this ability is called *gravitropism*. Without this, if you planted seeds upside down, the plant wouldn't grow. Plants detect gravity by dense material in their cells called *amyloplasts*. The amyloplasts are heavy so they sink to the bottom of the cells, telling the plants which way is down.

WHAT ELSE YOU CAN DO

● Instead of completely inverting the seedlings, try turning them horizontally and observe the influence of gravity.

● Make several seed germinators and investigate the effects of additives to the water, such as fertilizer, acid rain, or other pollutants.

● Modify the brightness, color, and duration of light to see how these influence seed growth.

Making a Seed Germinator

WHAT YOU NEED

▶ **Empty 16 to 20-ounce (480 to 600 mL) plastic water bottle**

▶ **Craft knife**

▶ **Scissors**

▶ **Ruler**

▶ **CD jewel case**

▶ **Glue gun and glue sticks**

▶ **Paper towels**

▶ **Piece of tape**

▶ **Seeds (radish seeds work best)**

INSTRUCTIONS

1. Make a 5-inch (12.7 cm) cut with the craft knife along the long end of the empty water bottle. Use the scissors to widen the cut until you have a 5 x ½-inch (12.7 x 1.3 cm) rectangular hole in the bottle (figure 1).

2. Remove the black insert from the CD case. This will be the base of your seed germinator.

Figure 1

3. Hot glue the bottle to the black insert so that the hole in the bottle is facing straight up. The black insert base will keep the bottle from rolling (figure 2).

Figure 2

4. Fold two or three paper towels so they fill the inside of the CD case. The paper towels should lie flat against the deeper half of the CD case.

5. Fill the bottle about a quarter full with water. Make sure the cap is on tight!

6. Carefully place the CD case (with the paper towels inserted) into the bottle (figure 3). You may need to use the scissors to trim the hole in the bottle if it's difficult to insert the CD case.

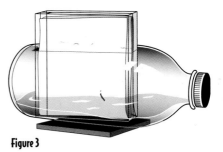

Figure 3

7. While the CD case is in the bottle, use the tape to mark 1 inch (2.5 cm) above the hole in the bottle.

8. Once the paper towel is completely soaked with water, remove the CD case from the bottle.

9. Open the CD case, and place 10 seeds on the paper towel at the 1- inch mark. Press the seeds firmly into the paper towel so they won't fall.

10. Gently close the CD case and place it back into the bottle (figure 4). If any of the seeds fall, remove the CD case and replace them.

Figure 4

Cloche Encounters

Some gardeners like to get a head start on their veggies and plant them before the last frost. One way to do this is with *cloches*, which are like tiny greenhouses that sit over your plants at night. This experiment tests which cloche is best for your plants.

PROBLEM/PURPOSE

What's the effect of using glass, plastic, and paper cloches on spinach sprouts planted before the last frost?

EXPERIMENT SUMMARY

You'll use several cloches, which you'll put over young spinach plants in the garden. As nighttime temperatures plummet, watch to see which plants flourish and which flounder.

WHAT YOU NEED

▶ **5 plastic ½ gallon (1.9 L) opaque milk jugs**
▶ **Scissors**
▶ **Newspaper**
▶ **Gardening tools**
▶ **Spinach sprouts or seeds**
▶ **Plant pots and gardening soil (optional)**
▶ **5 large glass jars**
▶ **Thermometer**

EXPERIMENTAL PROCEDURE

1. Contact your local Cooperative Extension Agency to find out the date of the last frost in your area. Frost is a deposit of ice crystals that forms when water vapor condenses as temperatures dip below freezing.

Frost can damage tender plants, and the colder the temperatures, the more damage you can expect.

2. Find a flat, 5-foot-square (1.5 m) area in your garden that gets the same amount of sunlight. This will require a bit of observation. If you plant your sprouts in an area where some plants will get more sunlight than others, this will affect your experiment. The amount of sunlight each plant receives needs to be a constant for this experiment to work.

3. To make the plastic cloches, cut off the bottom 2 inches (5.1 cm) of the plastic milk jugs. Make five of these.

4. To make the paper cloches, fold two newspaper pages into a rectangle (figure 1). Bring two opposite corners of the folded side together down the center to form a triangle (figure 2). Roll up the long rectangular edge that remains at the bottom to form a brim (figures 3 and 4). Open it up and you've got a cloche.

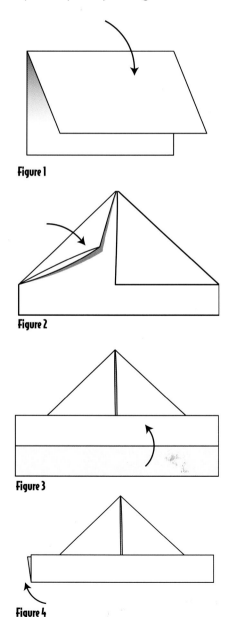

Figure 1

Figure 2

Figure 3

Figure 4

5. Make five of the paper cloches. To put one over a plant, load soil into the brim of the hat so it won't blow away. The glass jars are the last set of cloches.

6. You can usually find spinach sprouts in garden centers and even home improvement centers well before the last frost in your area. If not, grow your spinach indoors from seeds, and then transplant them for your experiment. Start early and plant more seeds than you need for the experiment.

7. Plant 15 sprouts 1 foot (30.5 cm) apart in the spot you picked in step 2. If the ground is frozen, plant the sprouts in pots indoors and then place them outside in their pots.

8. In the soil near the plants, mark which cloche will cover each one: plastic, paper, and glass. There should be five plants for each type of cloche. Place the thermometer in the garden near the cloches.

9. Each evening (when the temperature is supposed to drop below freezing) place the cloches over the sprouts.

10. Each night at the same time (like right before you go to bed), check the temperature outside with the thermometer. Record the date, time, and temperature.

11. Each morning before school, record the date, time, and temperature again. Remove each cloche and check for signs of frost damage, which could include wilting leaves,

brown leaves, and ice crystals on the plant. Record what you observe.

12. If the temperature stays below freezing during the day, leave the cloches on the plants when you're done checking on them. If not, take the cloches off the plants. If you can, have someone at home remove the cloches soon after the temperature rises above freezing. The cloches could actually burn your plants if you leave them on when it's warm out. (Then you'd have to start your whole experiment over.)

13. You don't have to water the plants very much, but when you do, make sure to water in the morning so your plants aren't spending the cold night in wet conditions. (They wouldn't like that anymore than you would.)

14. Observe how each sprout is doing each afternoon after school until the threat of frost has passed. Record your observations.

CONCLUSION

Which plants did best? There are variables to watch out for here. For instance, if you don't get the cloches off the plants during the day, the plants in the glass containers could roast, while the ones in the plastic containers may flourish. Cloches could also blow over during the night, exposing your plants. Make sure to record any of these things if they happen.

Touching Memories

People use all sorts of tricks to remember things. They repeat phone numbers in their heads over and over. They use the first letter of each item in a list to make up a word they can remember. But what about using touch to remember? Check it out.

PROBLEM/PURPOSE

What effect does touching an object have on one's ability to remember the object?

EXPERIMENT SUMMARY

You'll test the memory of your volunteers using common objects. During the first test, they'll try to memorize what they see by just looking at the objects. During the second test, your volunteers will also touch the objects.

WHAT YOU NEED

- ▶ 30 different household objects
- ▶ 2 tables in 2 different rooms
- ▶ 10 to 15 volunteers
- ▶ Paper and pencil
- ▶ Stopwatch

EXPERIMENTAL PROCEDURE

1. Spread out 15 objects on each table in two different rooms. They should all be different items but things that you can find around your home.

2. Ask your first volunteer to close his or her eyes and go into the first room. (Naturally, you'll have to lead the way.)

3. Instruct your volunteer to open his or her eyes when you say "start." Then, he or she will look at the table and try to memorize as many objects as possible without touching them.

4. Time the volunteer with the stopwatch for 30 seconds. Say "stop," and have your volunteer close his or her eyes again.

5. Take your volunteer into another room without any objects. Instruct him or her to write down the objects he or she remembers on a piece of paper. Give your volunteer 60 seconds to do this.

6. Ask your volunteer to close his or her eyes again and go into the second room with the second table of objects.

7. This time, your volunteer should look at and touch the objects as he or she tries to memorize them. Say "stop" after 30 seconds, and have your volunteer close his or her eyes.

8. Take your volunteer into the room without any objects. Instruct him or her to write down the objects he or she remembers on a piece of paper. Give your volunteer 60 seconds to do this.

9. Repeat steps 2 through 8 with all of your volunteers.

10. Average the number of objects your volunteers remembered from each table.

CONCLUSION

Show your results in a data table. You may also want to display them in a line graph. Were the objects memorized more easily with touch or without? What other factors could have affected your volunteers' ability to memorize the objects in this experiment?

TAKE A CLOSER LOOK

◉ Memory is usually categorized into *short-term* (or *working*) *memory* and *long-term memory*. Whether or not you store something in your short-term memory may be influenced by what you associate with it. For example, if you're looking at a red toy car, you may remember it if you have a red car. As well, if you interact with the toy car in some way, you may remember the object later.

◉ Information enters our short term memory through the five senses. The more senses involved in receiving information, the more likely we are to remember it.

WHAT ELSE YOU CAN DO

◉ Instead of touching the objects, instruct the volunteers to say the name of each object out loud for the 30-second interval.

◉ Ask the volunteer to list the objects from each table again the next day to see if they can still remember them. (Don't tell them you're going to do this ahead of time!)

Hair-Raising Strength

In the fairy tale, Rapunzel used her hair as a rope ladder. Would she have been better off as a blonde or a brunette?

Adult Supervision Required

PROBLEM/PURPOSE

What effect does hair color have on its strength?

EXPERIMENT SUMMARY

You'll test various colored hairs to see if there's a difference in the amount of weight each can hold.

WHAT YOU NEED

▶ **Strength tester (see page 47)**
▶ **Paper clip**
▶ **Small plastic bag**
▶ **6-inch (15.2 cm) pieces of hair from a salon in four or more different colors**
▶ **Tape**
▶ **Small marbles**
▶ **Balance***

Ask your science teacher if you can borrow one.

EXPERIMENTAL PROCEDURE

1. Make the strength tester. See the following page. With the paper clip, make a small hole near the top of the plastic bag. This is your weight basket.

2. Tape one end of the first piece of hair to the middle of the vertical dowel piece (see illustration). Loop the hair around to the other side, and tape the other end.

3. Hook the plastic bag to the loop of hair using the paper clip.

4. Add marbles to the plastic bag one at a time until the hair breaks.

5. Record in your data table the number of marbles it took to break each hair you tested.

6. Repeat steps 2 through 5 several times with each color of hair.

7. Measure and record the mass of your marbles with the balance. Figure out how much weight each piece of hair held.

CONCLUSION

Which hair color was the strongest? How much weight did each hair color hold? Show your results in a bar graph.

TAKE A CLOSER LOOK

● Hair is made of a fibrous protein called *keratin*. Nails and the outer layer of skin are also made of keratin.

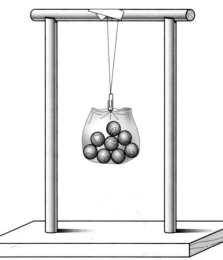

● A single strand of hair can hold approximately 2.8 ounces (78.4 g), while a rope of 1,000 strands can hold up to 175 pounds (79.4 kg)!

● *Melanocytes* are the cells that determine what color your hair is. They are also located in skin and produce pigments called *melanin*. There are two types of melanin: *eumelanin* is present in brown, brownish-black and black hair; *pheomelanin* is present in blonde and red hair.

Your hair turns gray or white when your body stops producing melanin.

WHAT ELSE YOU CAN DO

● Treat one type of hair with various shampoos or chemicals, then perform the strength test.

● Look at the different hair colors under a powerful microscope. Are there differences in the cross-sectional shape?

Making the Strength Tester

WHAT YOU NEED

▶ **Small wooden dowel**

▶ **Small saw**

▶ **Block of wood (approximately 6 x 12 inches [15.2 x 30.5 cm])**

▶ **Drill**

▶ **Hot glue or wood glue**

INSTRUCTIONS

1. Get an adult to cut the wooden dowel into three pieces: two 12 inches (30.5 cm) long and one 9 inches (22.9 cm) long.

2. Cut a V shape in the top of both 12-inch (30.5 cm) pieces so that you can lay the 9-inch (22.9 cm) piece horizontally across the top (see illustration on page 46).

3. Have an adult help you drill a small hole into the block of wood. It needs to be wide enough to hold one 12-inch (30.5 cm) dowel piece. Use the glue to hold the dowel upright.

4. Have an adult help you drill another hole 7 inches (17.8 cm) away from the first. Glue the second 12-inch dowel in the hole.

5. Lay the 9-inch (22.9 cm) dowel piece across the top of the two 12-inch (30.5 cm) pieces. Glue it to hold it in place.

Nursery Rhyme and Fairy Tale Science Fair Project Quiz

Take a break from your science fair project, and see if you can match up the nursery rhyme or fairy tale with its science fair project. For example, "Four and 20 Blackbirds" would be paired up with this problem: "How many blackbirds can really fit into a pie?" Umm…by the way, don't try these at home! Answers appear below.

Story or Rhyme

1. Cinderella
2. Diddle, Diddle Dumpling, My Son John
3. Goldilocks and the Three Bears
4. Humpty Dumpty
5. Itsy Bitsy Spider
6. Jack & Jill
7. Little Jack Horner
8. Little Red Riding Hood
9. Mary Had a Little Lamb
10. Peter Piper
11. Princess and the Pea
12. The Emperor's New Clothes
13. The Three Little Pigs
14. Twinkle, Twinkle, Little Star
15. Little Miss Muffet
16. The Three Billy Goats Gruff
17. Jack and the Beanstalk
18. Snow White and the Seven Dwarfs
19. The Pied Piper
20. Chicken Little

Problem/Purpose

A. What percentage of the time will you run into a wolf if you take a shortcut through the woods?

B. What factors can cause sleep disorders?

C. What effect does bowl size have on how quickly porridge cools off?

D. How do scientists tell what stars are made of?

E. How do spiders survive rainstorms?

F. Which shoes provide the best traction for hilly terrain?

G. What materials best protect eggs from cracking?

H. How would the combination of mass and velocity affect a goat's ability to knock a troll off a bridge?

I. Which brand of plum pie has the most plums?

J. If you picked a peck of pickled peppers, what percentage of picked pickled peppers…where was I?

K. Can glass be used as an effective material for making shoes?

L. What effect do curds and whey have on spiders' appetites?

M. How powerful is the power of suggestion?

N. What's the best fertilizer for a beanstalk?

O. How can rumors cause needless panic?

P. Which building materials hold up best against strong winds?

Q. How can animals be trained to follow you around?

R. How do human's measure beauty?

S. How does music affect a rat's performance in a maze (especially flute music)?

T. How will sleeping with one shoe off and one shoe on affect sleeping patterns?

Answers:
1, K; 2, T; 3,
C; 4, G; 5, E; 6,
F; 7, I; 8, A; 9, Q;
10, J; 11, B; 12, M; 13, P; 14, D; 15,
L; 16, H; 17, N; 18, R; 19, S; 20, O

Bow-Wow Blood Pressure

Blood pressure is the force of blood against the blood vessel walls. This pressure keeps the blood circulating in the bodies of various organisms. We know that a person or animal's overall health affects blood pressure, but what about their overall size?

PROBLEM/PURPOSE

How does the size of a dog affect its blood pressure?

EXPERIMENT SUMMARY

Spending the day at a local vet clinic, you'll be able to observe many different sized dogs and compare their size (height and weight) and blood pressure.

WHAT YOU NEED

▶ **A local veterinarian clinic**

▶ **Paper and pencil**

EXPERIMENTAL PROCEDURE

1. Call a local veterinarian clinic, and ask to speak with a vet. Tell him or her you're working on a science fair project. Explain your hypothesis and that you would like to spend a day or two with him or her in the office recording the weight, height, and blood pressure of many different-sized dogs.

2. Record the weight, height and blood pressure of as many dogs as possible in your visits. If this isn't possible, perhaps the veterinarian

would record this information for you.

3. Make two line graphs, comparing height versus blood pressure on one and weight versus blood pressure on the other.

CONCLUSION

Is there any correlation or relationship between the height of the dog and its blood pressure? What about the weight and its blood pressure? Does the pressure increase or decrease with weight or height, or does it vary?

TAKE A CLOSER LOOK

● Blood pressure is measured with an instrument called a *sphygmomanometer*. It measures pressure with the rise and fall of a column of mercury and expressed in millimeters of mercury (mmHg). It is usually given in two numbers. The first number, which is higher, is the pressure the heart puts on the major arteries when it contracts. The second number is the pressure of the blood vessel walls as they contract.

● Gravity affects blood pressure by pulling the blood to the lower part of

the body. Blood pressure helps keep the blood from pooling there. Here are some comparisons of blood pressure (first number only) for different-sized animals:

Animal	Blood pressure	Animal	Blood pressure
Human	120	Monkey	140
Duck	162	Pig	128
Cow	157	Snake	55
Horse	78	Giraffe	300
Cat	129	Frog	24
Crayfish	8	Guinea pig	60
Lobster	8		

WHAT ELSE YOU CAN DO

● Compare the pulse of various animals to their size.

● Compare the blood pressure of a dog before and after exercise.

● How does age affect a dog's blood pressure?

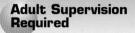

Compost Concoction

What is dirt? Well, a lot of it is worm poop—and worm poop is actually good for everybody.

PROBLEM/PURPOSE

How does adding worms to your compost affect soil fertility?

EXPERIMENT SUMMARY

You'll create two different composts, one with worms and one without, to determine which makes the best organic fertilizer.

WHAT YOU NEED

▸ **Two 10-gallon (38 L) buckets**
▸ **Drill**
▸ **Tape**
▸ **Permanent marker**
▸ **Ruler**
▸ **Small shovel**
▸ **Small bag of vermiculite**
▸ **Soil from your backyard**
▸ **Water**
▸ **Dead leaves**
▸ **Food scraps (no meat, dairy, egg shells, fat or oil)**
▸ **Two dozen red worms***
▸ **Soil fertility test kit****

*Available at a bait shop

**Available at a plant shop or nursery

EXPERIMENTAL PROCEDURE

1. Ask an adult to help you drill 10 small holes in the bottom of each bucket, and 10 small holes around the outside of each bucket. This will give the composting material the oxygen it needs to break down.

2. Label one bucket with the tape and marker as the worm bucket. Leave the other bucket blank.

3. Add 2 inches (5 cm) of vermiculite to the bottom of each bucket.

4. Add soil from your backyard to each bucket until it is half full.

5. Add the same amount of water to each bucket. The soil should be just barely moist. Mix the water in with the shovel.

Record the amount of water you add and the date. You may need to add more water to the buckets throughout the experiment to keep the soil moist. Always record the amount, and add the same amount to each bucket.

6. Add a layer of dead leaves from your backyard, making sure you add the same amount to each bucket.

7. Next, add a layer of food scraps from your kitchen, such as fruit peels, vegetable matter, and bread. Be sure you add the same amount to each bucket.

8. Mix the leaves and food scraps into the soil with the shovel.

9. Add the worms to the bucket labeled worms.

10. Place the buckets outside in a place protected from rain or snow. Getting additional water in the buckets will affect your results. If you don't have a covered area, cover the buckets with a piece of wood or their plastic lids.

Yum...worms!

11. Add more food scraps and leaves every few days. Always add the same amount to each bucket and record the amount you added. Carefully mix in the scraps and leaves with the shovel. You should turn the soil over every time you mix in more water, scraps, or leaves.

12. Record any observations about the composts (appearance, temperature, smell, etc.), along with the amounts of scraps, leaves, and water added, on your data sheet.

13. After one month, test the fertility of the soil using the test kit. Follow the instructions that came with the kit. You will be testing the amount of nutrients in the soil and the pH of the soil. Determine which compost was most effective at creating fertile soil that could be used in a garden. If you can't get a kit, simply plant some seeds using the different types of soil, and compare growth.

CONCLUSION

Which bucket contained the most fertile soil? Did the scraps in the soil with the worms decompose faster? Create a data table showing your results.

TAKE A CLOSER LOOK

● Composting is a way to take advantage of the decomposition of organic matter such as leaves and vegetable matter and recycle it back into soil. Bacteria and fungi play an important role in this process, as they feed on the nutrients from the decaying matter. Worms can also play an important part by breaking the organic matter down and aerating the soil, giving it more oxygen. It's also a great way to reduce the amount of garbage your family throws away!

WHAT ELSE YOU CAN DO

● Turn the soil in one bucket every three days and not the other. See which one decomposes faster. (Don't put worms in either of the buckets.)

● Measure the temperature of the compost to find out the best temperature for decay.

Do You See What I See?

Depth perception is how you determine how far away an object is from you. Do you think this is a quality that will get better or worse as you get older?

?

PROBLEM/PURPOSE

What effect does age have on depth perception?

EXPERIMENT SUMMARY

Placing pencils at different distances from your volunteers, you'll test to see if their perception of depth is different based on their age.

WHAT YOU NEED

▶ **2 pencils**

▶ **Red tape**

▶ **Blue tape**

▶ **Paper**

▶ **Ruler**

▶ **Book or box**

▶ **Table**

▶ **2 chairs**

▶ **At least 10 volunteers of different ages**

EXPERIMENTAL PROCEDURE

1. Tape the eraser end of one pencil with blue tape and the other with red.

2. On a piece of 8½ x 11-inch (21.6 x 27.9 cm) paper, draw a 2 x 1-inch (5.1 x 2.5 cm) rectangle in the middle of the paper. This will be the depth guide you'll use for testing each volunteer.

3. Sit at the table and hold the pencils with the erasers up. Use the book or box to hide your hands so the volunteer will not see them. Place the other chair 8 feet (2.4 m) away from the table. You may need to place books under the pencils so that the volunteer can see the tops of the pencils. The tops of the pencils should be at eye level for the volunteer.

4. Begin testing by placing the two pencils on any two corners of the rectangle you drew. Ask the volunteer to tell you if the red or blue pencil is closer or are they at the same distance. Record his or her answer (correct or incorrect) on your data sheet. Don't tell the volunteer if he or she is correct or not until you're finished with the entire testing procedure.

5. Repeat steps 3 and 4 with each volunteer 5 times. The volunteer should close his or her eyes in between each test so he or she won't see you shift the pencils. Repeat the question, "Which is closer?" as you shift the pencils to various points on your rectangle and record answers on your data sheet.

CONCLUSION

Calculate the percentage of times each volunteer got it correct. Figure out the percentage of correct answers for each volunteer using the following formula:

Percentage correct = number correct ÷ number possible x 100

Which age group had the highest percentage of correct answers? Did the age of the person affect their depth perception? Could there be other factors affecting depth perception? If so, what do you think they might be?

TAKE A CLOSER LOOK

● If you close one eye, what you see is the *visual field* for that particular eye. Now open your eye and close the other one. Do you see how the visual fields for both eyes overlap in the middle? The overlapping allows your brain to judge the depth of objects in the total visual field. Tah-dah—depth perception!

● Animals often have their eyes spread farther apart than ours. They don't have a lot of overlap in their visual fields, but they can watch out for predators better. How do you think this might affect their depth perception? How does eye placement differ on predators and prey? Why do you think that might be?

WHAT ELSE YOU CAN DO

● Test depth perception of each eye individually, instead of both eyes by instructing the volunteer to cover one eye.

● Test depth perception with the volunteers seated at varying distances from the pencils. On average, at what distance do most people lose their depth perception?

Don't Hold Your Breath!

Your heart pumps the oxygen from your lungs to all of the cells in your body. But what does your heart do if your lungs are taking a coffee break?

PROBLEM/PURPOSE

How does breathing affect your heart rate?

EXPERIMENT SUMMARY

You'll measure your heart rate after hyperventilating and hypoventilating to observe the effect of breathing on heart rate.

WHAT YOU NEED

▶ **Stopwatch**

▶ **Paper and pencil**

▶ **5 volunteers***

*Warning: Anyone prone to dizziness, nausea, or headaches should not be used as a test subject. Keep an adult nearby to assist with this project.

EXPERIMENTAL PROCEDURE

1. Practice measuring your heart rate before collecting data. Place your index and middle finger together on your neck a couple of inches below your ear and just behind your jaw bone. You should feel a slight pulsing just below your skin. This is the blood moving through your arteries as your heart pumps. Each pulse is a contraction of your heart. Use the stopwatch to count how many pulses you feel in 10 seconds. This is your heart rate. You should have about 10 to 15 pulses in 10 seconds (or 60 to 90 beats per minute) if you are sitting still. This is called your *resting heart rate*.

2. Repeat step 1 until you feel comfortable measuring your heart rate. Record your resting heart rate. This will be your control heart rate.

3. Hold your breath as long as you can. Breathe normally for 30 seconds, and hold your breath again. When you are done holding your breath, immediately take your heart rate. Record this as your *hypoventilating heart rate*.

4. Rest for about 5 minutes so your heart rate returns to normal.

5. Take shallow breaths or pant for 30 seconds. Breathe normally for 30 seconds and then pant for another 30 seconds. Immediately take your heart rate. Record this as your *hyperventilating rate*.

6. Repeat steps 3 through 5 at least six times so that you can get a good average value for your hypo- and hyperventilating heart rates. Remember to rest between each measurement. Your heart rate should return to its resting rate.

7. After you've tested yourself, repeat steps 1 through 6 with each of your volunteers. When your volunteer first comes into the room, have him or her sit in a comfortable chair and relax for up to 15 minutes. This will insure that the first pulse you take is the volunteer's resting heart rate.

CONCLUSION

Make a bar graph of the average resting, hyperventilating, and hypoventilating heart rates. Which had the lowest value? Which had the highest value? How is heart rate influenced by breathing?

TAKE A CLOSER LOOK

● During *hyperventilation*, your breathing rate is greater than what is needed for a proper exchange of oxygen and carbon dioxide. You're taking in more oxygen than your body needs, causing your heart rate to increase so that the blood will circulate more quickly to use the incoming oxygen.

● During *hypoventilation*, your lungs are using up the same amount of oxygen even though you're taking less air in. This causes a buildup in carbon dioxide levels, which makes your heart rate decrease.

WHAT ELSE YOU CAN DO

● How does body position, such as sitting, standing, lying down, or standing on your head, affect heart rate?

● How does your heart rate vary during different times of the day?

● How do other factors, such as age, height, weight, or physical fitness, affect heart rate?

Physical Science

"Please stop rolling your marbles down my map. We'll cover kinetic energy next week."

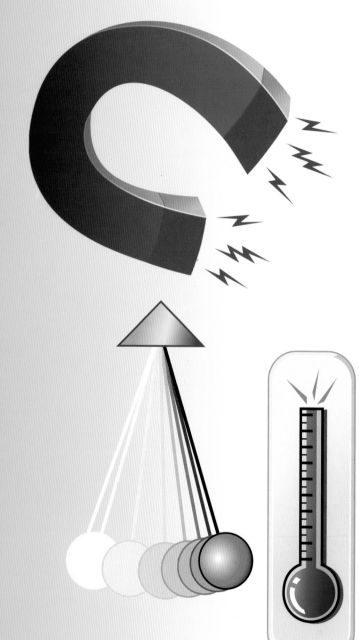

If biology is the study of life, then physical science is the study of stuff that's not alive. From parachutes to pollution, physical science studies it all. This topic covers nature, weather, water, magnets, stars, planets, environmental concerns, engineering, physics, and more. Curious about the air in your bicycle tires? What's in the cereal you're eating? How much trash your family creates? Then keep reading.

The Attraction of Traction

Why do runners run on special surfaces? And why can't you wear your street shoes on the gym floor?

PROBLEM/PURPOSE

How does the surface you're running on affect your speed?

EXPERIMENT SUMMARY

You'll measure the amount of time it takes for someone to run the same distance on a gym floor, track, in the grass, and on sand.

WHAT YOU NEED

▶ Volunteer
▶ Gym floor
▶ Stopwatch
▶ Tape measure
▶ Track
▶ Grassy area
▶ Sandy area

EXPERIMENTAL PROCEDURE

1. Take your volunteer, with his or her running shoes, to the gym. Mark a starting line on the floor, and have the volunteer stand behind that line.

2. When you say "go," start the stopwatch and have the volunteer start running as fast as possible.

3. After 5 seconds, tell the volunteer to stop running.

4. Measure the distance the volunteer ran with the tape measure. Record the distance.

5. Repeat steps 2 through 4 at least two more times on the gym floor.

6. Go to the track, and repeat steps 1 through 5.

7. Find a nice, flat, grassy area, and repeat steps 1 through 5.

8. Go somewhere flat with sand, and repeat steps 1 through 5. (If you don't live near a beach, you could skip this step.)

CONCLUSION

On what surface did the volunteer run the farthest? Make a chart of your observations. How did the different surfaces affect how far the volunteer ran?

TAKE A CLOSER LOOK

● *Friction* is the force that resists movement between two bodies. Different surfaces have more or less friction than others: for example, a slick surface will have less friction than a rough, bumpy one.

● Gym floors are designed to be used for many different sports. The floor is very slick for some shoes (like street shoes) but not for others (like basketball shoes).

● When you're running on sand, the sand particles move underneath your foot as you push off. This means that some of your energy is being used to move the sand instead of being used to move you.

Parachute Power

Without parachutes, skydiving would be an even more dangerous sport than it already is. How do parachutes work? And does the shape of a parachute determine whether or not you'll have a gentle landing?

PROBLEM/PURPOSE

How does the shape of a parachute affect how long it will stay in the air?

EXPERIMENT SUMMARY

You'll create several different-shaped parachutes, then drop them all from the same height and see how long it takes each one to reach the ground.

WHAT YOU NEED

- ▶ **Templates on page 109**
- ▶ **Plastic garbage bags**
- ▶ **Scissors**
- ▶ **Ruler**
- ▶ **Hole punch**
- ▶ **String**
- ▶ **4 corks**
- ▶ **16 thumbtacks**
- ▶ **Stepladder**
- ▶ **Helper**
- ▶ **Stopwatch**

EXPERIMENTAL PROCEDURE

1. To make the parachutes, use the templates on page 109 to cut the parachute shapes out of the plastic bags. (Each shape has the same surface area so this doesn't become a variable in your experiment.)

2. Use the hole punch to make four holes in each parachute for the strings.

3. Cut 16 pieces of string, each 24 inches (30.5 cm) long and tie each one through one of the holes in the parachutes. Tie the ends of each parachute string to the thumbtacks. Push the thumbtacks into the corks.

4. Have your helper climb the stepladder with the first parachute. She should hold the parachute away from her body with her arm straight out in front of her.

5. Instruct your helper to drop the parachute when you say, "Go." Time the parachute's descent with the stopwatch. Record how long it takes for the parachute to reach the ground. Repeat nine times. Average your results.

6. Repeat steps 4 and 5 with the other three parachutes.

CONCLUSION

Which parachute stayed in the air the longest? Why do you think that is? Show your results in a bar graph. Did the parachutes float differently? In what way?

TAKE A CLOSER LOOK

● The *rate of descent* is the measurement of how quickly a parachute falls. Air resistance makes a parachute float. The pressure of the air against the parachute slows the pull of gravity on it.

● *Aerodynamics* describes the interaction between the air and the parachute. Although each parachute shape has the same area, not all parachute shapes work equally well. (See the next page for more information.)

WHAT ELSE YOU CAN DO

● Test how one parachute shape responds to different string length.

● How does the material you make the parachute out of affect its rate of descent?

What a Drag!

The next time you go skydiving, take a moment to consider some of the key laws of physics at work while you plummet back to earth. (Yeah, right!)

The first thing you'll probably notice is gravity. In fact, you'll notice it as soon as you step out of the plane. Yes, you're falling. And yes, those are tears of fear getting the insides of your goggles all wet.

The second thing you'll notice is how scared you are thinking about the fact that you're falling. This is not a law of physics, just something to consider the NEXT time you decide to jump out of an airplane.

Next, there you are just falling. But you're accelerating! At this point gravity is stronger than the *drag* (the friction) between you and the air. So, you'll notice that you're falling faster and faster. As you speed downward, the amount of drag increases (the faster something falls, the greater the drag). That's a good thing.

Finally, as drag becomes equal to gravity, you're no longer falling faster. You're just falling at a constant speed. You've reached your *terminal velocity*. And, yes, if you hit the ground at this speed, it will be terminal. But here's some good news. You won't fall any faster than you are now. Oh, by the way, you're falling at about 125 miles per hour (200 km).

Umm…open your parachute, please.

Thanks to your open parachute, you now have a much larger surface area and a lot more friction between you and the parachute and the air. Yes, you've also got a lot more drag. Perfect timing. And you'll feel the deceleration caused by drag. In fact, your upward force is now temporarily greater than the force of gravity. You seem to stop before continuing your descent.* And this time, you're slowing down. You keep slowing down until once again drag and gravity are equal. Your constant velocity is now around 14 miles per hour (22 km). Just slow enough to make a safe landing.

*If you watch someone skydiving on television or in a movie, it looks like the person shoots straight up right after opening his or her parachute. This is an optical illusion. The camera operator is still falling at the same rate as before, so it looks like the skydiver has shot up.

Gauge Your Tires

The tires on your bicycle give you recommended levels of air pressure, but what level of air pressure will give you the greatest speed?

PROBLEM/PURPOSE

What effect does bicycle tire pressure have on speed?

EXPERIMENT SUMMARY

You'll test your bike speed over a 50-meter (165-foot) course with different tire pressures. Air pressure is measured in pounds per square inch (psi) or kilopascals (kPa). (The formula to make the metric conversion is 6.9 kPa = 1 psi.)

WHAT YOU NEED

▶ Chalk
▶ Tape measure
▶ Bicycle
▶ Bike pump
▶ Tire gauge
▶ Helper
▶ Stopwatch

EXPERIMENTAL PROCEDURE

1. Find a flat area and mark a starting line with the chalk.

2. Measure exactly 50 meters (165 feet) to the finish line. Mark that

point with the chalk. (This experiment is much easier to conduct using metrics.)

3. Ask your assistant to time your ride. If you have a multi-speed bike, don't change gears at any point during this experiment. Doing so will introduce a variable into your experiment.

4. Let the air out of the tires until you have 50 percent less than the recommended pressure in each tire. (Take the recommended pressure and divide by two to figure out how much pressure should be in your tires.)

5. Get on your bike and approach the starting line. Have your timer yell, "Go!"

6. Accelerate as quickly as possible to the finish line.

7. Record the time it took to get to the finish line.

8. Repeat two more times with the same air pressure, and average the times.

9. Fill your tires to the recommended pressure, and repeat steps 5 through 8.

10. Fill your tires 25 percent over the recommended pressure (multi-

ply the recommended pressure by 1.25), and repeat steps 5 through 8.

11. Fill your tires 50 percent over the recommended pressure (multiply the recommended pressure by 1.5), and repeat steps 5 through 8.

CONCLUSION

To determine your speed, take the number of meters and divide by the number of seconds it took to travel the distance. For example, if it took you 20 seconds to travel 50 meters, the equation would be 50 ÷ 20 = 2.5 meters per second. The part of the tire that touches the road is called the *contact patch*. The amount of air in your wheels determines how big your contact patch is. The more tire you have touching the ground, the more resistance is created. Which pressure gave you the best average time? Which pressure would you recommend to someone about to embark on a race?

TAKE A CLOSER LOOK

● What's the air in your tire actually doing? The air atoms are colliding with the sides of the tire at incredible speeds. These collisions exert a pressure outward. The more air you add to the tire, the more collisions you're creating and the greater the pressure. What do you think would happen to those air atoms if you increased or decreased the temperature? What happens to your bike tires after spending a winter out in the garage?

WHAT ELSE YOU CAN DO

● Instead of acceleration, you could compare air pressure and braking distance.

● You can measure the contact patch by putting a piece of paper under the bike tires. Sit on the bike and have your assistant trace the tires. Compare the area to the average speed and air pressure.

● Why might you want to inflate your tires less for riding off-road than if you were riding on-road?

● What happens to air pressure when temperature changes? Take three basketballs and fill them with the same amount of air pressure. Make sure they all bounce to the same height. Put one basketball in the freezer (if it fits), keep one at room temperature, and put one in the attic (if it's hot) or in the trunk of the car (or anyplace that's a lot warmer than room temperature). After several hours compare the bounces of the balls.

Crunch Your Breakfast

Does the idea of sinking your teeth into a nice bowlful of iron (with a little milk on top) sound like the perfect way to get you moving in the morning? Chances are, this is exactly how you get started every day.

Which cereals have the most iron?

EXPERIMENT SUMMARY

You'll use a magnet to test how much iron has been added to different cereals.

WHAT YOU NEED

- ▶ **Several different types of cereal**
- ▶ **Measuring cup**
- ▶ **Cereal bowls**
- ▶ **Masking tape**
- ▶ **Permanent marker**
- ▶ **Water**
- ▶ **Wooden spoon**
- ▶ **Strong magnet***
- ▶ **Scale (optional)**
- ▶ **Duct tape**

* You can buy one at a hardware store.

EXPERIMENTAL PROCEDURE

1. Pour 2 cups (210 g) of each different type of cereal into separate bowls. Label the bowls with the type of cereal they contain, using the tape and permanent marker.

2. Add enough water to cover the cereal in the first bowl. Let the water soak in until the cereal is nice and mushy.

3. Stir the cereal vigorously with the wooden spoon for 5 minutes. Put the bar magnet in the cereal, and stir it for a few more minutes.

4. Let the mixture stand for 10 minutes. Then, remove the magnet, and slowly pour the cereal mush out.

5. Look at your bar magnet. Do you see little black needles and specks? That's the iron. Estimate how much of the bar magnet is covered with iron. Record your results. (If you can borrow a scale from your science teacher, weigh the iron.)

6. Rinse off the bar magnet and the spoon. Use the duct tape to remove any iron specks still on the magnet. Repeat steps 2 through 6 with each bowl of cereal.

CONCLUSION

Make a bar graph showing how much iron you found in the different cereals.

TAKE A CLOSER LOOK

● Iron is added to many cereals because it's something we need to have in our diets. Your body uses iron for many things, but most importantly, red blood cells use iron to carry oxygen to all of the cells in your body.

● The iron in cereal is the exact same iron in nails and cars. Tiny pieces of it are mixed into the cereal batter. The hydrochloric acid in your stomach and intestines react with the tiny particles of iron you eat and change them into a substance that you can digest.

Feel the Burn

Did you get a sunburn the last time you went to the beach? What kind of sunscreen did you use? Could you have used a more powerful kind and saved yourself from a nasty burn?

PROBLEM/PURPOSE

Which sunscreens work the best?

EXPERIMENT SUMMARY

You'll put sunscreen over photoreactive paper to determine which SPF (sun protection factor) value blocks the most sun rays.

WHAT YOU NEED

▶ Sheet of 8½ x 11-inch (21.6 x 27.9 cm) acetate*
▶ Scissors
▶ Ruler
▶ Permanent marker
▶ ⅛ teaspoon (.6 mL) measuring spoon
▶ SPF 8 sunscreen**
▶ SPF 15 sunscreen**
▶ SPF 30 sunscreen**
▶ Photoreactive paper***
▶ Cookie sheet
▶ Bowl of water

*These clear plastic sheets are available at paper supply stores or copy centers.

**Use the same brand of sunscreen.

***Available at some science supply stores and toy stores, and over the Internet (see page 111).

EXPERIMENTAL PROCEDURE

1. Cut the sheet of acetate into four quarters. Label the pieces SPF 8, 15, 30, and 0 with the permanent marker.

2. Measure out ⅛ teaspoon (.6 mL) of SPF 8 sunscreen. Use your fingers to evenly spread all of the sunscreen over the transparency labeled SPF 8. Wash and dry your hands when you're through.

3. Repeat step 2 for the SPF 15 and SPF 30 sunscreen. Leave the transparency labeled SPF 0 bare.

4. Read the instructions on the photoreactive paper. Quickly and carefully remove the photoreactive paper from its protective envelope, and place four pieces on the cookie sheet. Immediately cover the sheets with the four transparencies.

5. Place the cookie sheet with the papers and transparencies out in the sun. Make sure the cookie sheet is in the full sun. Any shadow that blocks part of the cookie sheet will alter your results.

6. When the paper labeled SPF 0 is almost white (1 to 4 minutes depending on the intensity of the sunlight), bring the cookie sheet inside.

7. Carefully take the transparencies off, and use the permanent marker to label each piece of paper with the appropriate SPF. Throw the transparencies away.

8. Rinse the papers in the bowl of water for 1 minute to fix the sunprint, or follow the instructions on the package if they specify that you do something else.

9. Lay the papers flat to dry.

CONCLUSION

Follow the instructions for setting the photoreactive paper, and then compare the color of each sheet of paper and record your results. Which SPF blocked the most sunlight? Which SPF blocked the least? Are your results what you expected? Graph the sunscreens from least to most protective.

TAKE A CLOSER LOOK

● The sun emits many types of radiation. Our skin cells absorb ultraviolet radiation. When the cells absorb the radiation, it causes damage and can lead to skin cancers. Sunscreen absorbs and reflects these damaging rays before they have a chance to interact with skin cells.

● Correctly applied sunscreen with an SPF of 15 reduces the UVB exposure by more than 90 percent. However, people rarely apply sunscreen as often as recommended, so the SPF actually achieved is usually less than half of the advertised value.

WHAT ELSE YOU CAN DO

● Sunscreens come in a variety of types, brands, and SPFs. Compare PABA free (para amino benzic acid—part of vitamin B complex) versus sunscreens containing PABA.

● Compare expensive brands of sunscreen to more affordable ones. Which work better?

● See if you can locate bottles of sunscreens from last summer or earlier. Are sunscreens less effective as they age?

● Some dermatologists claim that anything above SPF 30 is not necessarily more effective at protecting you from the sun. Is there a difference between SPF 30, 45, 50, and higher?

Do You Smell What I Smell?

Have you ever been at a gathering when all of a sudden you caught a whiff of perfume? Were you able to figure out whose perfume it was? Where was that person standing?

PROBLEM/PURPOSE

How does the way perfume particles move through the air affect when people in a room smell them?

EXPERIMENT SUMMARY

You'll blindfold three volunteers and time how long it takes each person to smell perfume sprayed in the room.

WHAT YOU NEED

▶ **3 volunteers of the same sex and age**
▶ **3 blindfolds**
▶ **Perfume in a spray bottle**
▶ **Measuring tape (optional)**
▶ **Stopwatch**

EXPERIMENTAL PROCEDURE

1. Find a room in which to conduct your experiment. Make sure that there are no open windows or drafts, and that any heating or air conditioning is turned off. Anything that affects the airflow in the room will influence your experiment.

2. Blindfold your volunteers, and tell them to quietly raise their hands when they smell the perfume.

3. Stand your volunteers in a line, each one about 5 feet away from the person in front of him or her. Stand a good distance back from your volunteers. Spray a bit of the perfume into the air as you start the stopwatch.

4. Each time a volunteer raises his or her hand, record the time showing on the stopwatch.

5. When all the volunteers have smelled the perfume, measure the distance between where you sprayed the perfume and where the volunteers were standing.

6. Repeat steps 3 through 5, each time putting your volunteers in a different arrangement.

CONCLUSION

When you arranged your volunteers in different ways, who smelled the perfume first? Are your results what you expected? Why or why not?

TAKE A CLOSER LOOK

● Gas molecules always move from areas of higher concentration to areas of lower concentration. This is called *diffusion*. So, when you spray the perfume, it's in an area of higher concentration (there's a lot of perfume in one place). Soon after, the perfume molecules move to areas of lower concentration (anywhere else in the room).

● Molecules are moving around in every direction all the time. Air molecules are constantly bumping into each other and bouncing around. When another gas diffuses into the air, the gas molecules get bumped around and moved through the air that way.

The Way the Ball Bounces

Thanks to the laws of physics, we can play soccer, basketball, baseball, volleyball, and more. Gravity pulls the ball to the ground, and the ball's potential and kinetic energy bounce the ball back to you. This experiment tests how height affects how the ball bounces.

PROBLEM/PURPOSE

How does the height from which you drop a ball affect how high it bounces?

EXPERIMENT SUMMARY

You'll drop a ball from various heights and measure how high it bounces.

WHAT YOU NEED

▶ **Hard, flat surface**
▶ **Basketball (or some other ball that bounces)**
▶ **2 yardsticks**
▶ **Masking tape**
▶ **Wall**
▶ **Stepladder or stool (optional)**
▶ **Helper (optional)**
▶ **Video camera (optional)**

EXPERIMENTAL PROCEDURE

1. Find a hard, flat surface on which to bounce your ball.

2. Use the tape to secure both of the yardsticks against a wall or other vertical support. Tape one above the other so that you can measure 6 feet (1.8 m) above the ground.

3. Drop the ball from 6 feet (1.8 m) above the ground. This means the top of the ball should start at the top of the second yardstick. You may need a stool or stepladder to reach this high. If you have a helper, have him or her drop the ball for you.

4. Carefully observe the height that the top of the ball reaches at the highest point of the first bounce. Record your results. You may wish to videotape the bouncing ball to make this measurement easier.

5. Repeat the measurement at least five times at this height and calculate the average value.

6. Repeat steps 3 through 5 at: 5 feet (1.5 m), 4 feet (1.2 m), and 3 feet (.9 m).

CONCLUSION

Make a line graph of the drop height versus the average bounce height. What is the relationship between these heights? Calculate the ratio of bounce height versus drop height. Is this value the same for the four bounces you measured?

TAKE A CLOSER LOOK

When you hold the ball in the air, it's full of *potential energy* (or energy of position). When you drop the ball, the potential energy is converted to *kinetic energy* (or energy of motion). As it bounces back up, the kinetic energy is converted back into potential energy. However, the ball will not return quite as high as you dropped it since some of the energy is transformed into heat and sound in the collision with the floor.

If you drop the same ball on the same surface, the height it bounces back to will be the exact same relative to the height you drop the ball from. In other words, if you drop the ball and it bounces back to half the height from which you dropped it, when you drop it again from the halfway height, it will bounce a quarter of the way back. This is called the *coefficient of restitution*. Inflation will affect the coefficient of restitution.

The next time you watch a basketball game, pay careful attention to the referee when he receives the game ball. You will see him drop the ball from shoulder height, and watch how high it bounces. A regulation ball should bounce up to his waist when dropped from shoulder height. If the ball bounces too low or too high, it cannot be used in an official game.

WHAT ELSE YOU CAN DO

Investigate the bounce of different types of balls such as soccer, tennis, golf, baseball, or other balls that bounce.

See how balls bounce on different surfaces such as concrete, gymnasium floor, grass, clay tennis courts, and others.

How does inflation affect the way a ball bounces? Can you overinflate a basketball?

How does temperature affect the bounce of a ball? Do hot or cold balls bounce higher?

Blockheads

Sand (as well as crushed gravel, river rock, and even crushed shells) can be added to cement and water to make concrete. Sand provides the bulk that gives concrete its strength. Does the size of sand grains affect the strength of concrete?

PROBLEM/PURPOSE

How does the size of sand grains affect the strength of a concrete block?

EXPERIMENT SUMMARY

You'll make three different blocks or bricks, using three different sizes of sand, and test the strength of each one.

WHAT YOU NEED

▶ **Small-, medium-, and large-grain sand***

▶ **Measuring cup**

▶ **Bowl**

▶ **White craft glue**

▶ **Fork**

▶ **Plastic wrap**

▶ **Rectangular soap molds****

▶ **Stack of books**

▶ **Pound (or metric) weight set**

Check with local concrete manufacturers in your area for sand you can use.

**Available in the soapmaking section of craft stores*

EXPERIMENTAL PROCEDURE.

1. Measure ⅓ cup (80 g) of the fine sand and put it in the bowl. Add ⅛ cup (30 mL) of the white craft glue, and stir the mixture together with the fork.

2. Line the rectangular soap molds with the plastic wrap. This will make it a lot easier to get the bricks out.

3. Press the mixture into one of the soap molds. Press it down with the fork to make sure that no air gets in the brick.

4. Repeat steps 1 and 2 with each of the sizes of sand. Make at least two of each type of brick. (The more the better!)

5. Let all of your bricks harden in the molds. Let them sit for three days, then take them out of the molds. Let them sit until they are completely hard. This may take another five days or so.

6. Make two stacks of books on a table. They should be close together so that you can set one of the bricks between them. The brick should overlap about 1 inch on either side of the books.

7. Start putting weights on top of the first brick. Increase the weight by the smallest increment possible. When you run out of that weight, replace the weights on the brick with a larger one weighing the same amount. For instance, put 1-pound (.5 kg) weights on top of the brick until you have five of them on the brick. Then replace the five 1-pound (.5 kg) weights with a 5-pound (2.5 kg) weight and start adding the 1-pound (.5 kg) weights one at a time again. Continue to add weight until your brick breaks.

8. Record how much weight your brick held before it broke.

9. Repeat steps 7 and 8 with each brick.

CONCLUSION

Average the weight each of the bricks made of small sand particles could hold. Do the same for the bricks made of medium, large, and mixed sand particles. Which bricks held the most weight? Show your results in a bar graph. What are the practical implications of this?

TAKE A CLOSER LOOK

● When actually making concrete, builders will often prefer a well-graded mix of sand or gravel to provide extra strength. That means including various sizes. Why? The smaller pieces shift to fill in spaces between larger ones, so that when cement coats each piece and hardens into a solid mass, there are less holes and more mass.

Take a Closer Look
Squashing Pumpkins

Every year on October 31 at 11 am (more or less), the West Virginia University Student Chapter of the American Society of Mechanical Engineers (whew!) sponsors a Pumpkin Drop. Why would a bunch of engineering students want to throw a bunch of pumpkins from 11 floors high just to watch them squash to pieces? I know, silly question. But, while there is a certain amount of joy to be had watching large gourds get tossed off a rooftop, this contest isn't that simple. There's a catch to this event. The idea is to throw your pumpkin off the top of the Engineering Sciences Building and not only get it closest to the target 11 floors below, but also to devise some sort of contraption to keep your pumpkin from incurring any harm from the impact (i.e. squashing). The closest unharmed pumpkin to the target wins. Ahh, now the "engineering" part makes sense, doesn't it!? The challenge of coming up with a container that gets the pumpkin to the ground (while in free fall) without it going splat isn't as easy as it sounds. Every year only around 10 percent of the 150 pumpkins tossed "overboard" make it unharmed.

Hmm.... Any practical implications at work here? How about you register for the Pumpkin Drop; invent a cost-effective, environmentally friendly, compact design; win the contest; and sell your design to the post office for big bucks? Not a bad idea. Or, do all the above, and contact the World Pumpkin Deliverers Association (if there is one).

Want to try this at home, but afraid of any laws (or family rules) you might be breaking? Organize an egg drop instead. All you need is a ladder, some cool egg-protecting contraptions, and a bunch of eggs. While you're at it, check out the Association of Mechanical Engineers. They sponsor an Egg Drop competition every spring.

Popcorn Fever

You're watching your favorite movie, curled up on the couch with a huge bowl of popcorn. Everything is great, until you reach into the bowl for a big handful of the fluffy popcorn and end up with a mouthful of unpopped kernels. Yuck!

PROBLEM/PURPOSE

How does the temperature at which you store microwavable popcorn affect how well it pops?

EXPERIMENT SUMMARY

You'll store microwavable popcorn in the freezer, refrigerator, and on the counter for 24 hours. Then you'll pop the popcorn and see how many kernels are left unpopped in each bag.

WHAT YOU NEED

- ▶ **16 bags of microwavable popcorn**
- ▶ **Permanent marker**
- ▶ **Freezer**
- ▶ **Refrigerator**
- ▶ **Measuring cup**
- ▶ **Water**
- ▶ **Microwave**
- ▶ **Cookie sheet**

EXPERIMENTAL PROCEDURE

1. Label each bag of the popcorn with the permanent marker. Label the first five bags: freezer 1 through 5. Label the next five bags: refrigerator 1 through 5. Label the last five bags: counter 1 through 5. Don't label the last bag of popcorn.

2. Put the bags labeled "freezer" in the freezer and the bags labeled "refrigerator" in the refrigerator. Put the bags labeled "counter" on the counter. Put the last bag with these.

3. Wait 24 hours before continuing your experiment.

4. Fill the measuring cup with 1 cup of water, and put it in the microwave on high for 1 minute. This will preheat the microwave oven for you. Take the measuring cup out of the microwave, and dry it out.

5. Put the unmarked bag of popcorn in the microwave. Set the microwave on high for 5 minutes. Listen carefully. When the popping rate slows to 2 to 3 seconds between each pop, stop the microwave. Note exactly how long the bag was in there.

6. Take the first bag of popcorn out of the freezer, and put it in the microwave. Set the microwave to the time you determined in step 5.

7. Take the bag out of the microwave, open it, and measure the popcorn using the measuring cup. Record the volume of the popcorn.

8. Pour the popcorn onto the cookie sheet. Separate the unpopped kernels and count them. Record the number of unpopped kernels.

9. Repeat steps 5 through 8 for each bag of popcorn.

CONCLUSION

Average the results for the five bags of popcorn that were in the freezer. Do the same for the popcorn in the refrigerator and on the counter. What storage temperature resulted in the most unpopped kernels? What storage temperature had the least? How was the volume of the popcorn influenced? Did the bags of popcorn with the fewest unpopped kernels have the most volume? Why or why not?

TAKE A CLOSER LOOK

● Popcorn pops because of three elements: the starch and moisture inside the kernel, and the hard shell surrounding the kernel.

● When the moisture inside the kernel heats up, it expands. When it expands so much that the shell can no longer hold it in, the popcorn pops.

● There's no white on the inside of popcorn. The white, fluffy part is what happens to the starch when it's heated. The starch expands, forming thin, jelly-like bubbles. The starch bubbles fuse together with the ones around them, and then you've got popcorn.

WHAT ELSE YOU CAN DO

● What would happen if you pierce the shells of unpopped kernels with a straight pin?

Pollution Dilution

Pollution isn't just the garbage you kindly pick up off the sidewalk. There's also the light pollution we here on Earth create that makes it difficult to see the night sky.

Adult Supervision Required

PROBLEM/PURPOSE

What effect does light pollution have on your ability to see stars?

EXPERIMENT SUMMARY

You'll test how light affects the number of stars you can see by counting them in different locations.

WHAT YOU NEED

▶ **4 x 6-inch (10.2 x 15.2 cm) picture frame**
▶ **A moonless night**
▶ **Adult helper**
▶ **Paper and pencil**

EXPERIMENTAL PROCEDURE

1. Take the glass, photograph, cardboard insides, and backing out of the picture frame, so you're left only with the frame.

2. Wait until it's completely dark (9 pm or later) before starting this experiment. Find the darkest place in your neighborhood. Bring along an adult and the picture frame.

3. Wait 15 minutes to let your eyes adjust, and then look up and locate the Big Dipper. Make sure you don't look at any bright lights during this 15-minute period.

4. Place your picture frame at arm's length up in the air, and center a part of the Big Dipper inside the frame. Count how many stars you see. Record the number.

5. Find a place that isn't as dark—perhaps near a street light. Repeat steps 3 and 4.

6. Go to the center of your hometown or to a parking lot in front of a grocery store that stays open late. Repeat steps 3 and 4.

7. Repeat these steps at least one more time.

CONCLUSION

Did the number of stars you counted around the Big Dipper change? Where did you see the most stars? Where did you see the least? Why do you think that is?

TAKE A CLOSER LOOK

● Light pollution keeps us from being able to see as many stars as we would otherwise see. Light pollution is what happens when artificial lighting is misdirected or overused. Light bounces up into the atmosphere, creating a glow around big cities. This glow makes the light coming from the sky much dimmer and harder to see. Astronomers are finding it increasingly difficult to see the sky, and some observatories located near cities are now more or less useless.

DISPLAY TIPS

If you want, check your neighborhood to see how people use lights. Are any houses totally illuminated all night? How many lit billboards are there along the roads in your hometown? Take pictures of light pollution and use them in your display. The pictures may not look terrific, but they'll get the point across.

Starry night? Hard to tell with all these lights! These two photographs courtesy of Robert D. Miller.

The Reasons for the Seasons

Ask all the smart people in your life why we have seasons. If any of them say it's because we're either closer or farther away from the Sun, do this experiment to see whether they're right or wrong.

PROBLEM/PURPOSE

What causes the seasons?

EXPERIMENT SUMMARY

You'll mimic the tilt of the Earth by placing pieces of black cardboard with thermometers attached to them at different angles.

WHAT YOU NEED

▶ Black paint and a paintbrush
▶ 3 pieces of cardboard
▶ Tape
▶ 3 thermometers
▶ Rocks or bricks to prop up cardboard

EXPERIMENTAL PROCEDURE

1. Paint the three pieces of cardboard black. Once the cardboard pieces are dry, tape one of the thermometers to the center of each piece of cardboard.

2. Place the cardboard pieces in the shade until the thermometers read the same temperature.

3. Place all three pieces of cardboard in the sun. The first one should be propped up by rocks or bricks until the Sun is hitting the thermometer straight on. Lay the second piece a little farther backward. Lay the third cardboard piece flat on the ground or slightly tilted backward.

4. Check and record the temperatures every couple minutes.

CONCLUSION

What did you notice? Imagine that each piece of cardboard represents the Earth. Which Earth is the hottest? Coolest? How can that help explain the seasons?

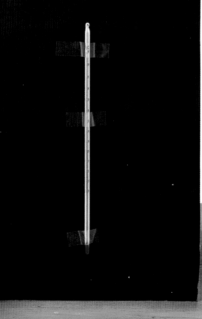

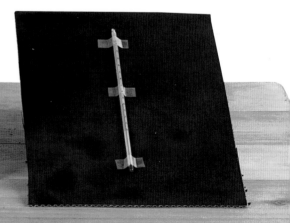

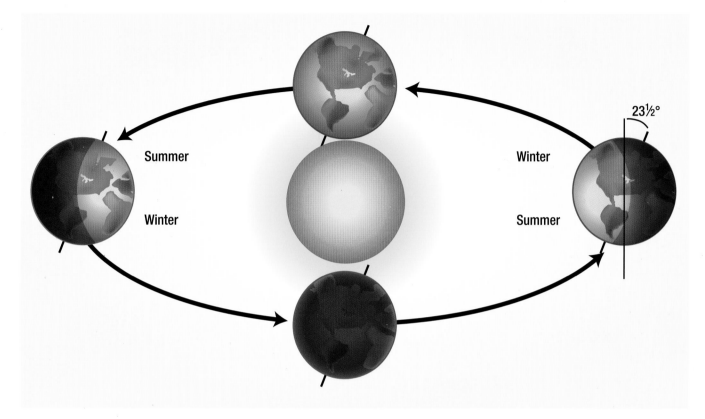

Summer

Winter

Winter

Summer

23½°

TAKE A CLOSER LOOK

● The *angle* of the sunlight influences the amount of energy it creates. Light rays hitting straight on are strongest. At an angle, light spreads out and is less intense. This not only explains why it's hotter around noon than it is early in the morning or later in the evening, but also why it's winter in the northern hemisphere while it's summer in the southern hemisphere. How? Take a look at the illustration above.

As Earth rotates, it's tilted about 23½ degrees, instead of being straight up and down like a spinning top. This changes the angle at which sunlight hits the surface as Earth makes its yearly journey around the Sun. The northern hemisphere gets more sunlight when Earth is tipped toward the Sun, so it's hotter (summer). At the same time, the southern hemisphere is tilted away from the Sun. The sunlight spreads out

more thinly over a greater area there, so it's colder (winter). Also, days are longer in the summer and shorter in the winter, so when it's winter, not only are you receiving less intense sunlight, you're also receiving sunlight for less time.

● Because the equator is in the middle of the Earth, it receives pretty much the same amount of light all year round. There is no winter there; it's summer all year long.

The Radical Reduce Refuse Plan

Garbage stinks. Yet, no matter how much we hate it, we keep making it. Turn your next science fair project into a family affair as you research how you can make a difference in the amount of garbage that ends up in the landfill.

PROBLEM/PURPOSE

?

How much can one family reduce their garbage in three months?

EXPERIMENT SUMMARY

This is a four-week experiment. During the first week you'll figure out how much garbage your family produces, and during the next three weeks, you'll attempt to reduce the amount of garbage you make.

WHAT YOU NEED

▶ **Scale**

▶ **Gallon-sized (4 L), self-sealing plastic bags**

▶ **Large plastic garbage bags**

▶ **Latex gloves**

EXPERIMENTAL PROCEDURE

1. Get your whole family involved in this experiment if possible. For the first week, place two garbage bags in the kitchen. One will be for food items, while the other one will be for "dry" garbage. Tell your family to put their garbage in either of those two bags for the whole week.

2. Give each member of your family two gallon-sized (4 L), self-sealing plastic bags: one for food, one for "dry" garbage. It's important to get your family members to agree to place ALL garbage they'd normally throw away outside the home (at work, school, etc.) in the gallon-sized (4 L) bags. This includes left-over lunch and cola bottles, but doesn't include tissues and toilet paper. When you get home, put your garbage in the bigger bags. Wash out the smaller bags every night for them, and have them reuse the bags the next day. (Hey, it's the least you can do.)

3. After the week of garbage collecting, weigh yourself and record your weight. Then weigh yourself holding the dry garbage bag. Subtract your weight, and you have how many pounds of dry garbage your family produced. Do the same thing for the food garbage bag. Add the weight of the two garbage bags together for a total amount.

4. Put on some latex gloves, and go through the garbage with your family. Discuss ways to eliminate most of the garbage. Devise a plan, and implement it (see Tips for Your Family).

5. Once the plan is put into action, make sure your family sticks to it. Make sure they keep their garbage baggies with them, and continue to weigh your garbage at the end of each week. Do this for as long as your family will let you. Try for a month. (Hey, try for forever!)

6. After the agreed-upon amount of time has passed, do a final weigh-in.

CONCLUSION

How much did your garbage decrease? Did the decrease continue throughout the experiment? How many pounds of garbage did you eradicate from the landfill?

TAKE A CLOSER LOOK

⬤ The average person throws away more than 4 pounds (1.8 kg) of trash each day.

⬤ Packaging alone makes up 64 million tons (58 million metric tons) by weight, or 33% of all our garbage.

⬤ A family that reduces their garbage saves resources, energy, and disposal costs.

DISPLAY TIPS

Display your results, and show how much garbage can be reduced if every house on your block did the same thing. What if every family in the country followed this plan?

TIPS FOR YOUR FAMILY

⬤ Start a compost bin in the backyard for food scraps and uneaten leftovers.

⬤ Use sponges and rags instead of paper towels.

⬤ Use cloth napkins.

⬤ Reuse plastic food containers to store leftovers instead of aluminum foil and plastic wrap.

⬤ Let the companies that send you junk mail know that you don't want it. Look on the Internet for ways to eliminate junk mail.

⬤ Buy in bulk.

⬤ Buy items that can be recycled.

⬤ Bring along canvas bags or reuse plastic bags when you go shopping.

⬤ Don't just throw away scrap paper. Use the other side, and then recycle it.

Keeping Warm

When the temperatures start dropping, it's time to put on more clothes. What kind of clothes will keep you the warmest?

PROBLEM/PURPOSE

How do different materials insulate?

EXPERIMENT SUMMARY

You'll measure how well different materials hold in heat.

WHAT YOU NEED

▶ **2 identical glass bottles**

▶ **Hot water**

▶ **2 thermometers**

▶ **Plastic wrap**

▶ **Wool socks**

▶ **Cotton socks**

EXPERIMENTAL PROCEDURE

1. Completely fill both bottles with hot water. Get ready, you must do steps 2, 3, and 4 quickly to get good results.

2. Quickly dry off the outside of each bottle. Place a thermometer in the opening of each bottle and seal the top with plastic wrap.

3. Cover one bottle with a wool sock, and leave the other bottle bare.

4. When the temperature in each bottle stops rising, record this as the initial temperature.

5. Let the bottles sit for 30 minutes. Record the final temperature.

6. Repeat steps 1 through 5 using a wet wool sock.

7. Repeat steps 1 through 5 with a dry cotton sock. Then do it again with a wet one.

CONCLUSION

How did the insulating properties of the wool sock and cotton sock compare? Which sock kept the most heat in the bottle? How did the insulating properties of wet and dry socks compare?

TAKE A CLOSER LOOK

● Cotton *wicks*, which means it draws water up the very small individual fibers, retaining the water and spreading it over the entire body. This causes a loss of body heat. Wool repels water and does not wick, so it is a nat-ural insulator that keeps you warm in the winter and cool in the summer. An ideal insulator would wick water away from your skin and dry quickly.

● Air is the best insulator, which is why "fluffy" materials like goose down (feathers) are used in winter coats.

● Engineers who design artificial fabrics, such as polar fleece, make fibers that are hollow so that air provides most of the insulation.

WHAT ELSE YOU CAN DO

● What other materials could you try? Try putting a bottle in the sleeve of your winter coat.

The Heating of Land and Water

It's the beginning of summer, and it's so hot at your house you're about to melt. After much begging, pleading, and bribing, you convince SOMEONE to take you to the beach. You're psyched—until you get there and discover that the water is really cold. You should have brought a wet suit.

PROBLEM/PURPOSE

How do lakes and oceans absorb heat compared to deserts and fields?

EXPERIMENT SUMMARY

You'll create models of a desert and a lake with sand and water. Then you'll measure how long it takes the sand and water to heat up and cool down.

WHAT YOU NEED

- ▶ 2 pans or pie tins
- ▶ Sand
- ▶ Water
- ▶ 2 thermometers
- ▶ Ruler
- ▶ 2 gooseneck lamps with 100-watt bulbs
- ▶ Stopwatch

EXPERIMENTAL PROCEDURE

1. Fill one pan ½ inch (1.3 cm) deep with sand and the other a ½ inch (1.3 cm) deep with water.

2. Place a thermometer in each tray so that the tip is under the surface of the sand or water. (You may want to lean the upper part of the thermometer against the side of the pan so you can still read the temperatures.)

3. Place a lamp about 4 inches (10.2 cm) above each tray. Each thermometer should be the same distance from the lamp. Do not turn the lamps on yet.

4. Record the initial temperatures of the sand and water. These values should be about the same.

5. Turn on the lamps and let them shine on the pans. Start the stopwatch, and record the temperatures of the sand and water every 2 minutes until 30 minutes has passed.

6. Turn off the lamp to let the trays cool. Record the temperatures of the sand and water every 2 minutes until the 30 minutes has passed.

CONCLUSION

Make a bar graph of temperature versus time for the water and the sand as it heated and then cooled. How did the temperatures of the sand and water change while they were heating and cooling?

TAKE A CLOSER LOOK

● Water heats up more slowly than sand for several reasons. The Sun's rays penetrate deeper into the water, and, since water is a fluid, it can spread the heat more evenly within itself. Water also needs more energy to raise its temperature, which means it has a higher *specific heat*. Specific heat is the amount of energy required to raise the temperature of a substance by one degree Celsius. Finally, some of the energy from the water is used to evaporate water from the surface, so less of the energy is used to heat the water.

● Air in the *troposphere* (bottom layer) is heated from the bottom up by heat given off by the surface. If the Sun shines equally on Seattle, Washington (near water) and Bismarck, North Dakota (near the center of the continent), Bismark would

heat up more quickly during the day. Seattle is affected by the ocean, which heats more slowly than the continent, but retains its heat for longer. This means that Bismark will also have a bigger difference between its day and night temperatures.

WHAT ELSE YOU CAN DO

● Would wet sand heat and cool the same as dry sand?

● How do different soils or different colored sands heat and cool?

● Does salt water heat and cool the same as fresh water?

● Does the depth of the water matter?

● How does this relate to the direction of ocean-shore breezes during the day and at night?

Crystal Creation

Crystals are made up of atoms that have a very specific structure. The shape of the crystal itself is a reflection of the atoms' chemical structure. That structure is repeated over and over again to form the crystal.

PROBLEM/PURPOSE

How does temperature affect the growth of crystals?

EXPERIMENT SUMMARY

You'll grow crystals in three different temperatures to see which grows fastest and largest.

WHAT YOU NEED

- Sewing thread
- 3 craft sticks
- Scissors
- 3 glasses or jars
- 3 paper clips
- Masking tape
- Permanent marker
- Water
- Use of a stovetop
- Metal pan for heating water
- Measuring cup and spoon
- Alum*
- Stirring spoons
- Heating pad
- Refrigerator
- Magnifying glass
- Small ruler with millimeters

*Available in the spice section of the grocery store

EXPERIMENTAL PROCEDURE

1. It may take a week or so for crystals to form, so plan your experiment ahead of time. Tie a piece of sewing thread to the middle of each of the three craft sticks.

2. Rest the craft stick across the top of a glass. Cut the thread so that each thread is long enough to hang down without touching the bottom.

3. Tie a paper clip to the end of each thread. This will serve as a weight for the thread.

4. Label each glass with tape as follows: #1, Room temperature; #2, Refrigerator; #3, Heating pad.

5. Heat 2 cups of water in the pan. Do not bring the water to a boil.

6. Dissolve as much alum in the water as possible, stirring in 1 teaspoon (5 g) at a time. When the alum won't dissolve anymore, you'll see a few grains left in the bottom of the pan. Stop adding alum, and record how much you put in.

7. Remove the solution from the stove. Add more alum, and stir until no more will dissolve. This is called a *supersaturated solution,* because it contains more *solute* (alum) than *solvent* (water).

8. Let the solution cool. Pour the same amount of it into each glass.

9. Place a craft stick over the top of each glass. The thread should be suspended in the solution with the paper clip holding it down.

10. Place #1 in a spot away from direct sunlight where it will not be disturbed. Place #2 in the refrigerator. Place #3 on the heating pad on low setting .

11. Observe each glass every day.

Hold up the craft sticks, and look at the threads with the magnifying glass. Record the amount, size and shape of any crystals you see. Continue observations until every jar has some crystal growth.

CONCLUSION

Which jar had the quickest crystal growth? Which jar had the largest crystals? Did the temperature have any effect on the growth of the crystals? Which temperature do you think is best for growing crystals? What other things might affect the growth?

TAKE A CLOSER LOOK

● When the solute is in the solution, it is attracted to other solute molecules. As the water evaporates, more and more solute molecules find each other and begin to clump together to form crystals, in a process called *precipitation*. The thread provides a place for the solute molecules to meet.

WHAT ELSE YOU CAN DO

● There are many salts that will grow crystals. Try experimenting with different ones and see which grows the largest or clearest crystals.

Take a Closer Look
Help! I'm Being Pelted by Space Junk!

You probably know that shooting stars are really *meteors* (small pieces of space junk entering our atmosphere and burning up). And perhaps you recall that anything that doesn't burn up and lands on Earth is called a *meteorite*. But did you know that you, your family and friends, your bike, your house, your dog, and just about everything else gets pelted by tons of *micrometeorites* a day?

So why aren't we protecting ourselves from this space junk with full body armor and stainless steel umbrellas? Well, for one thing, micrometeorites are just what they sound like: tiny particles of space junk. In fact, the largest micrometeorite is about the size of the dot on this "i".

And although you can search your whole life and not find a meteorite, micrometeorites are a cinch to find. They're everywhere. Here are some tips for locating your very own micrometeorites:

● Since meteorites and micrometeorites can be either rock, metal (nickel and iron), or a mixture of both, your best bet is to look for metallic ones with a magnet.

● Set up a bucket at the end of a drain spout. Rainwater will wash all sorts of particles off the roof, and you can collect them at the spout. To find the metallic micrometeorites, remove the obvious earth junk (leaves, branches, etc.), dry off what's left, and place the dried-off stuff on a piece of white paper. Place a magnet under the paper, and tilt the paper so the non-metallic garbage drops off.

● To find out if your metallic particles on your paper are actually micrometeorites, ask your science teacher if you can borrow a high-powered microscope. Particles from space will be rounded and have small dents or pits on their surfaces.

● Bring a bar magnet to the beach, and dump sand over it. Carefully wipe away any particles that stick to the magnet onto white paper.

● Place a bucket outside on a table during a rainstorm. Then put your magnet in the water or carefully pour the water in the bucket through a paper towel (have a friend help you hold the paper towel).

Happy hunting!

More on Space Junk

● Micrometeorites are made up from the leftovers of comets or debris from the formation of the solar system. The micrometeorites you find are about 4.6 billion years old.

● Thousands of visible meteorites hit the earth's atmosphere every day. Luckily, most of these meteorites burn up in the atmosphere (thanks to friction!), and whatever's left over (if anything) falls into the ocean. (Remember, there's a lot more water on earth than land.)

● Micrometeorites aren't the only things that fly in from outer space and pelt you every day. X-rays and gamma rays pulsating from stars and nebulae are zipping through the universe right now, and a lot of them are passing through you. In fact, by the time you finish reading this paragraph, four or five gamma rays will have done just that. These rays are like light in that they travel in waves. The difference is that gamma and x-rays have tiny wavelengths, so they've got lots of energy in them, and you can't see them without special equipment.

Chemistry

Although chemistry is a physical science, many science fairs like to give it its own section. Chemistry is the study of the different forms of matter. That means that chemists are curious about the structure, composition, properties, and reactions of gases, solids, liquids, and combinations of the three. Does slime fascinate you? In the mood to make a mummy? Want to study the reaction that makes dough rise? Well, then, you've come to the right place.

Al 27 — 13 ALUMINUM	**Mg** 24 — 12 MAGNESIUM	**C** 12 — 6 CARBON
H 1 — 1 HYDROGEN	**Ti** 48 — 22 TITANIUM	**Xe** 131 — 54 XENON

"Okay class, you all fail because none of you has your SAFETY GOGGLES on!"

Slimed!

Slime is great because it's, well, slimy. And here's a question of great scientific import: How slimy can slime be? It's up to you to find out! The world depends on it. Okay, maybe not, but slime sure is fun.

PROBLEM/PURPOSE

What effect do different amounts of laundry booster have on slime's viscosity?

EXPERIMENT SUMMARY

You'll create several homemade slimes using the same recipe, but changing the amount of laundry booster in each one. Then, you'll see which one is the slimiest (or the most *viscous*, if you want to be technical about it).

WHAT YOU NEED

▶ **Rubber gloves (optional)**
▶ **Several 4-ounce (120 mL) bottles of white craft glue**
▶ **Glass jar**
▶ **Water**
▶ **Spoon**
▶ **Food coloring (optional)**
▶ **Measuring cup**
▶ **Distilled water**
▶ **Glass bowl**
▶ **Teaspoon**
▶ **Powdered laundry booster***
▶ **Resealable plastic bags**
▶ **Permanent marker**
▶ **Several bricks**
▶ **Piece of scrap board, approximately 1 x 2 feet (30.5 x 61 cm)****

**Borax brand laundry booster works great for making slime. Look for it in the laundry detergent section of your grocery store.

**Slime can permanently mess up wood, fabric, and carpet, so be careful where you put it. Slime will also destroy plumbing, so do not dispose of your slime down a drain.

EXPERIMENTAL PROCEDURE

1. If you're allergic to laundry powder, wear the rubber gloves while you do this project.

2. Pour all of the glue from one of the bottles into the jar. Fill the empty glue bottle with water, and add it to the jar. Stir the mixture with the spoon. (You can add food coloring here if you want to be festive—a few drops will do. Make sure to add the same number of drops to each slime recipe you concoct.)

3. Pour 1 cup (240 mL) of distilled water into the glass bowl (not the jar!), and add 1 teaspoon (5 g) of the laundry booster. Mix it together well.

4. Slowly add the glue mixture you made in step 2 to the bowl, stirring it as you do so. Place the thick slime that forms into your hand, and

knead until it feels dry. (There will be extra water in the bowl.) It will be wet, stringy, and messy at first. The more you play with it, the more it mixes together and becomes firmer and less sticky.

5. Store your slime in a resealable plastic bag in the fridge. With the permanent marker, write on the bag how much laundry booster you used.

6. Repeat steps 2 through 5 three times, adding one more teaspoon (5 g) of laundry booster to the recipe each time.

7. Use the bricks and the board to create a ramp to race the slime on. Stack the bricks under one end of the board, and rest the other end on the ground.

8. Put your slime samples at the top of the ramp. Let them slide down. Which one made it down first? Which one took the longest? Record your results.

CONCLUSION

A substance is considered *viscous* when it's sticky and doesn't flow. Which slime was the most viscous? How does the viscosity of the slime relate to how much laundry booster you put in? What effect does laundry booster have on viscosity? The first slime down the ramp is the least viscous, because it flows the fastest. The last slime down the ramp is the most viscous.

TAKE A CLOSER LOOK

● Sir Isaac Newton stated that liquids only change their viscosity in response to a change in temperature. (Water is liquid until you get it cold enough; then, it's solid.) That's true, except for what's known as non-Newtonian fluids.

They do not fit Newton's laws of how true liquids behave in response to temperature change. Quicksand, many pastes and glues, gelatin, ketchup, and slime are all non-Newtonian fluids.

● The reaction that makes this particular slime work is the bonding of polyvinylacetate (PVAC) molecules in the glue to the laundry booster (sodium tetraborate). The molecules (polymers) are long to begin with, and they are tangled, which is why the glue is so viscous. Once the laundry booster links up some of the molecules, it becomes even more viscous. Not all of the molecules hook up, though. The more that do, the more viscous it becomes, until it reaches a point where it barely flows at all. The amount of attachment that occurs among the PVAC molecules depends in part on the concentration of laundry booster.

WHAT ELSE YOU CAN DO

● Add mineral oil, powder, or calcium chloride (de-icer salt) to the original slime recipe. How do these substances affect the slime?

● Instead of using a 50 percent glue-water solution, try a 33 percent solution (one bottle of glue and two bottles of water) or a 66 percent solution (one bottle of glue and one half bottle of water).

I Need More Salt, Mummy!

The ancient Egyptians believed that you had to preserve your body after death in order to bring it with you to the afterlife. They mummified everything with *natron*, a salt solution found in the Natron River. They mummified people, cats, dogs, monkeys, gazelles, and birds. How about mummifying a fish for science?

PROBLEM/PURPOSE

How does the mixture of the salt solution affect the mummification rate of a fish?

EXPERIMENT SUMMARY

You'll test three different salt mixtures to see which one mummifies a fish best.

WHAT YOU NEED

▶ Adult helper
▶ 4 whole fish (head, skin, scales, organs, and all) from the grocery store
▶ Fillet knife
▶ Measuring tape
▶ Scale
▶ Resealable plastic bags (big enough to hold the fish)
▶ Salt
▶ Baking soda
▶ Permanent marker
▶ Laundry booster
▶ Rubber gloves

EXPERIMENTAL PROCEDURE

1. Have an adult help you "dress" all four of the fish. This means the fish need to be scaled and gutted with the fillet knife.

2. Record the weight and length of each fish.

3. Place one fish in a resealable plastic bag. Don't do anything else to it.

4. Place another fish in a new bag along with a ½ salt and ½ baking soda mixture. Pack the mixture into the gut cavity of the fish. Make sure there's enough to cover the fish completely. Label the bag with the permanent marker: ½ salt and ½ baking soda.

5. Place the third fish in a bag with just baking soda. Pack the baking soda into the gut cavity of the fish. Make sure there's enough to cover the fish completely. Label the bag with the permanent marker: 100% baking soda.

6. Place the fourth fish in a bag with a ½ salt and ½ laundry booster mixture. Pack the mixture into the gut cavity of the fish. Make sure there's enough to cover the fish completely. Label the bag with the permanent marker: ½ salt and ½ laundry booster.

7. After you've packed, sealed, and labeled all of the bags, wash your hands well. Place the bags in a cool, dry location.

8. After seven days, put on the rubber gloves and remove each fish from the bags. Brush off the excess mixtures. What do the fish look like now? How do they smell? Weigh and measure the fish. Record all of your observations.

9. Throw away the used mixtures, and refill each bag with the same mixture that was in it before. Remember to pack the mixture into the gut cavity of the fish, and make sure there's enough to cover the fish completely. Wash your hands well.

10. In another seven days, repeat steps 8 and 9. Seven days later, each fish (except for the first fish) should be mummified. Weigh and measure each fish. Record all of your observations.

CONCLUSION

Based on your results, which mixture is the most effective? Which is the least? Why did the fish weigh less and less as the mummification process continued? How much of the fish's body was made up of water?

TAKE A CLOSER LOOK

● Bacteria decompose all dead things. In the case of animals, bacteria eat all of the soft tissue on the body: skin, organs, cartilage.

● Mummification preserves the soft tissue by *desiccating* the body. Desiccation dries out the body, removing all fluids and stopping the decomposition process. How? Well, bacteria need water to live and eat. No water, no bacteria.

Take a Closer Look
More on Mummies

Not all mummies were made on purpose. There are a few different types of naturally occurring mummies. Scientists have made remarkable discoveries about the culture and diet of our ancestors by studying these accidental mummies.

Peat Bog Mummies

Peat bogs, which are wetland areas with lots of peat moss, will mummify a body. There's no oxygen in peat moss, so the bacteria that would decompose the body can't survive. Here are two of the many mummies found in peat bogs:

● The Lindlow Man was found in England. He was murdered about 2,000 years ago, but is so well preserved that scientists have figured out what his last meal was. And it's obvious that he had a haircut two or three days before he died. He is the only peat bog mummy that has a beard.

● The Yde Girl was discovered in Denmark. She was about 16 years old when she died 2,000 years ago, and she had red hair.

Ice Mummies

People who died in cold, high places have been mummified by freezing.

● Özti the Iceman is the oldest and most well-preserved mummy found. He died in the Alps 5,000 years ago. He was found with his tools, weapons, and a medicine kit.

● Juanita the Ice Maiden was discovered on top of a mountain in Peru. She was sacrificed by the Incans about 500 years ago, when she was between 12 and 14 years old. Her skin, hair, blood, organs, and even the contents of her stomach were preserved. The cloth that she was wrapped in still retains its color.

Desert Mummies

When people were buried in the desert during the winter, their bodies froze and dried out before they could begin to decompose. This phenomenon is especially common in the deserts of Central Asia. The salt in the sand helped dry out and mummify the bodies.

● The mummies found near Cherchen are better preserved than Egyptian mummies. They're between 3,000 and 4,000 years old.

● There's a mummified baby, with its baby bottle. (It was made from a sheep's udder.)

● Some of these mummies have red hair and are dressed in Celtic clothing. How'd they get there?

This 2,000-year-old mummy is known as the Tollund Man. He was discovered in 1950 in a bog in Denmark. Most scientists believe he was executed (he has a noose around his neck) after eating a ritual meal of cereal gruel. You can see his leather cap and the rope around his neck in this photo.

Yeast Feast

What's your favorite topping for fungus? Peanut butter and jelly or tuna fish? Yeast is a fungus that is essential to making bread.

PROBLEM/PURPOSE

How does temperature affect yeast's ability to produce carbon dioxide?

EXPERIMENT SUMMARY

You'll create several carbon dioxide catchers out of balloons and empty bottles. These will measure how much gas yeast produces at different temperatures.

WHAT YOU NEED

- ▶ **Measuring cup**
- ▶ **Water**
- ▶ **A pot**
- ▶ **Use of a stovetop**
- ▶ **Thermometer**
- ▶ **Balloon**
- ▶ **14 packets active dry yeast**
- ▶ **Sugar**
- ▶ **Measuring spoons**
- ▶ **1-liter flask or water bottle**
- ▶ **Cloth tape measure**
- ▶ **Pencil and paper**

EXPERIMENTAL PROCEDURE

1. Heat 1 cup (240 mL) of water on the stove. Place the thermometer in the heated water, and turn off the stove once the water reaches 80°F (26.6°C).

2. As the water is heating up, stretch out your balloon, blow it up, and let the air out. Do this several times. This will make it easier for the gas to push the walls of the balloon.

3. Quickly put one packet of the yeast and 2 tablespoons (30 g) of sugar in the measuring cup. Pour in 1 cup (240 mL) of the warm water, and let the sugar and yeast dissolve.

4. Pour the dissolved mixture into the empty bottle, and quickly attach the balloon to the bottle's mouth.

5. Wait 30 minutes. Measure the circumference of the balloon with the cloth tape measure. Record the measurement.

6. Wait another 30 minutes, and measure again to see if the yeast is still at work. Record the measurement.

7. Keep measuring every 30 minutes until the balloon stops inflating. If the balloon doesn't inflate at all, write down 0 as your result.

8. Empty and clean out the bottle, and repeat steps 1 through 7 at least one more time with the water at the same temperature. Use a new balloon each time. Make sure it's the exact same size and type of balloon as the last one you used.

9. Repeat steps 1 through 8 with the water at the following temperatures: 90°F (32.2°C), 100°F (37.8°C), 110°F (43.3°C), 120°F (48.9°C), 130°F (54.4°C), and 140°F (60°C). Do each temperature at least twice, and average your results. Don't worry if the balloon doesn't inflate at some temperatures. The hot water could have killed the yeast, and the colder water could be too cold to activate the yeast.

CONCLUSION

Use a bar graph to illustrate your results. Depending on the type of yeast you use, you may have to wait several hours before the balloon stops inflating.

TAKE A CLOSER LOOK

● Yeast is a fungus (a plant-like living organism) that eats sugar and starches in flour, changing them into carbon dioxide and alcohol. This is called *fermentation*. Warm water activates the yeast. Very hot water will kill it, while cold water doesn't provide enough kick for the yeast to do its job.

● Yeast cells are tiny—one packet of yeast contains billions of them.

● When the yeast in bread dough eats the sugar and starches in the flour, the fermentation makes the bread dough rise.

● Why do you punch the dough down when making bread? Punching the dough down mixes the warmer dough with the cooler dough on the outside edges. Punching also releases excess carbon dioxide and spreads out the sugar for the yeast to eat. This often leads to the dough rising again.

WHAT ELSE YOU CAN DO

● Use the optimum temperature from your results of this experiment to test whether or not different brands of yeast activate at the same temperature.

● Will the balloon inflate at the same rate (both in terms of the time it takes and the maximum circumference of the balloon) if flour is used instead of sugar?

● What would happen if you used baking soda?

● Try using different colas instead of sugar and water to activate the yeast. Try diet versus regular sodas.

Magic Sand

Have you ever played with Magic Sand? It's fascinating stuff. When dry, it looks like ordinary sand. Pour it in water, however, and you can mold it into shapes. Pour out the water, and your Magic Sand is completely dry.

PROBLEM/PURPOSE

?

What effect do hydrophobic materials have on an oil and water solution?

EXPERIMENT SUMMARY

You'll fill three bowls with water and vegetable oil. Then, you'll add regular sand and Magic Sand to two of the bowls. With a feather, you'll see which one removes the most oil from the water.

WHAT YOU NEED

▶ **3 glass bowls**
▶ **Measuring cup**
▶ **Water**
▶ **Vegetable oil**
▶ **Sand**
▶ **Magic Sand***
▶ **9 feathers**

You can order Magic Sand over the Internet (see page 111), or find it at science supply stores. Really good toy stores will also carry it.

EXPERIMENTAL PROCEDURE

1. Using the measuring cup, fill each of the glass bowls with the same amount of water. Add the same amount of oil to each bowl so that the oil forms a skin on top of the water.

2. Leave the first bowl alone.

3. Add 1 cup of regular sand to the second bowl.

4. Add 1 cup of Magic Sand to the third bowl.

5. Wait 15 minutes, then drag a feather across the top of the water in each bowl. Use a different feather for each bowl.

6. Wait 30 minutes, then repeat step 5, using a new feather for each bowl.

7. Wait 1 hour, then repeat step 5, using a new feather for each bowl.

8. Let the feathers dry, then see how much oil is coating each one. Record your observations.

CONCLUSION

Which feather was coated in the most oil? Which had the least on it? Estimate the percentage of oil covering each feather. How did the passage of time affect the amount of oil that covered the feathers? What possible applications could this experiment have?

TAKE A CLOSER LOOK

● *Hydrophobic* substances, like Magic Sand, have a molecular structure that repels water. The molecular structure of *hydrophilic* substances, like regular sand, attracts water.

● Magic Sand was developed to clean up oil spills in the ocean. When Magic Sand is sprinkled on floating petroleum, it mixes with the oil and sinks to the bottom of the ocean. This keeps the petroleum from washing up on beaches and harming wildlife. Unfortunately, Magic Sand has never actually been used for this purpose, possibly because it's really expensive to produce.

● Magic Sand won't ever freeze because it can't get wet. This would make it useful for burying utility lines in really cold places, like the Arctic Circle. That way, even when the

ground is frozen, the utility lines can still be accessed when they need to be repaired.

WHAT ELSE YOU CAN DO

● During the Exxon Valdez clean up, workers used nylon bags stuffed with human hair to soak up the oil. Try using hair stuffed in nylon stockings to clean up your oil. How much hair do you need? Does the color of the hair affect how much oil it will soak up?

DISPLAY TIP

● Bring regular and Magic Sand to your science fair, along with a couple of bowls and water. Have people walking by compare the properties of Magic Sand to those of regular sand. What happens when you put them in water and try to shape them? What happens when you take them out of the water?

It's a Stretch

Have you ever wondered about the amazing and wonderful properties of a rubber band (beyond, of course, the ability to shoot one across the classroom)?

PROBLEM/PURPOSE

How does temperature affect the stretch of a rubber band?

EXPERIMENT SUMMARY

You'll suspend a weight from a rubber band. Then, you'll expose it to different temperatures and observe what happens.

WHAT YOU NEED

▶ **Rubber band**
▶ **Scissors**
▶ **Weight set or washers**
▶ **Shoebox**
▶ **Ruler**
▶ **Pencil or dowel**
▶ **Refrigerator**
▶ **Hair dryer**

EXPERIMENTAL PROCEDURE

1. Cut the rubber band in half with the scissors.

2. Tie a weight or a washer to one end of the rubber band.

3. Try to find a shoebox in which the ruler fits comfortably. Place the shoebox on one of its smaller sides (see photograph) and fit the ruler inside the box. Poke a hole in the middle of the top of the box and thread the rubber band through this hole.

4. Tie the rubber band to the pencil or dowel, and make sure the weight tied to the other end of the rubber band swings freely. Your contraption is now ready.

5. Let the rubber band stretch for 3 minutes at room temperature. Then record its length with the ruler in the shoebox.

6. Put the shoebox in the refrigerator for 15 minutes.

7. Open the refrigerator door and measure the length of the rubber band. Touch the rubber band and see how it feels. Record your observations.

8. Use the hair dryer to heat the rubber band in the shoebox for 5 minutes. Measure the rubber band and record your observations.

CONCLUSION

Under what conditions did your rubber band have the most stretch? The least stretch? Is this what you expected? Why do you think it works this way?

TAKE A CLOSER LOOK

● Rubber is weird because, unlike most things, it contracts when heated. Most substances expand when they are heated, like the liquid in a thermometer. ⤸

● *Entropy* determines whether a material expands or contracts when it's heated. Entropy is a measurement of the orderliness of the molecules that make up a substance. Adding more energy (in the form of heat) makes the molecules move around more. When the molecules are arranged neatly, they push against each other and expand. Rubber molecules are made up of long, skinny *polymer chains*. When it's heated, sections of the polymer chain start to move around vigorously. The other ends of the chain have to contract to make room for the movement. For a demonstration of this principle, wiggle a long piece of string on your desk. See how the ends have to move closer together in order for the string in the middle to move further apart? That's how the polymer chains in a rubber band react to heat. If you place a rubber band over your lip and then stretch it out you can feel it get cooler. When you cool the rubber it expands AND when you expand the rubber it gets cooler.

● Rubber comes from trees that grow in South and Central America. The pre-Columbian people there used it to make balls, containers, and to waterproof their clothing. Today, we can produce synthetic rubber, and it has a wide variety of applications, from waterproofing clothing to tires to roads.

Take a Closer Look
Polymers: The Chain Gang

Polymers are chains of individual molecules bound together in long lines. The individual molecules are called *monomers*. There are many, many types of polymers. Some of them are naturally occurring, like wood, leather, cotton, and rubber. A lot of them are synthetic, like plastics. Here are just a few places that you see polymers every day: drink bottles, food containers, CDs, computers, shampoo, play dough, straws, hair spray, your toothbrush, chewing gum, bulletproof vests, bicycle tires, fireproof clothing, styrofoam cups, Frisbees, cell phones, parachutes, pantyhose, ladders, musical instruments, coolers, fishing line, diapers, fleece clothing, sponges, shower curtains, electronics, cars, your teddy bear, elastic, acrylic paints, balloons, film for your camera, fake leather, tents, backpacks, raincoats, basketballs, tennis rackets, the soles of your shoes, sport clothes, golf balls, carpets, glues, linoleum, countertops, snorkeling equipment, skis, swimming pools, life jackets, nets, air mattresses, duct tape, insulation, and ice cream.

If you link a bunch of paper clips together, you've got a reasonable approximation of what a polymer chain looks like. Each of the paper clips is a monomer. They are bound together end to end. You can wiggle the chain and all the little monomers will move around. Make a whole bunch of paper clip chains, jumble them up, and throw them on your desk. You've got a polymer!

The polymer chains cross-link (attach to the other polymer chains next to them) a little bit, but the cross-link bond is nowhere near as strong as the links between the monomers in the polymer chains. If you try to rip a plastic grocery bag, you'll notice that pulling it one way stretches the bag. You're pulling the polymer chains in the direction that they lie, so they stretch out. If you pull the other way, the bag will rip because you're pulling the polymer chains apart from the other polymer chains where they aren't bonded together as tightly. If you rip a piece of newspaper, a similar thing happens because newspaper is made of wood, a naturally occurring polymer.

In 1953, Hermann Staudinger won the Nobel Prize in Chemistry for demonstrating that polymers are long chains of monomers. His research on natural rubber has made it possible for scientists to synthesize polymers.

Balloonatics

When you got that beautiful balloon bouquet for your birthday, you swore you'd keep the balloons floating around in your room forever. But two days after your birthday, all of those balloons were lying on the ground, all wrinkly and sorry-looking. What happened?

PROBLEM/PURPOSE

How does the size of a molecule affect its ability to escape from a balloon?

EXPERIMENT SUMMARY

You'll inflate balloons using air and helium, and measure which keeps its volume the longest.

WHAT YOU NEED

▶ 6 regular latex balloons
▶ Helium gas source
▶ 5-gallon (19 L) bucket
▶ Water
▶ Yardstick
▶ Helper

EXPERIMENTAL PROCEDURE

1. Blow up three balloons with air and three balloons with helium, all to the same size.

2. To measure the volume of each balloon, fill the 5-gallon (19 L) bucket about half full with water. Measure the height of the water with the yardstick and record it.

3. Submerge a balloon completely in the bucket, and use the yardstick to measure the height of the water. Get an assistant to help you. Record the data.

4. Calculate the volume of the balloon. First, subtract the initial height of the water from the height of the water after you submerged the balloon in it. Second, calculate the area of the bucket by measuring the width of the bucket. Divide this number in half to get the radius of the bucket, and multiply it by 3.14. Multiply the height the water rises by the area of the bucket. This is the volume of the balloon.

5. Repeats steps 3 and 4 for each balloon. Record all the data and the time you made the measurements.

6. Repeat steps 2 through 5 every 4 to 8 hours for each balloon until the volume no longer changes or the balloon is completely deflated.

This may take several days.

CONCLUSION

Make a graph of volume (the water height) versus time for the air and helium balloons. Which balloons deflated the quickest?

TAKE A CLOSER LOOK

● Balloons are made of polymer chains. See page 96 for more information on polymers. The gases diffuse through the balloons because they can escape through the gaps in the polymer chains lying next to each other. Since helium contains smaller molecules than air, it diffuses faster.

WHAT ELSE YOU CAN DO

● Mix equal amounts of baking soda and vinegar in a bottle. Quickly stretch the opening of a balloon over the mouth of the bottle. When the balloon is full, tie it off and repeat the volume measurements. How does carbon dioxide compare to helium and air?

Shake It Up Baby!

If you perform this experiment, you'll be able to figure out how to maximize the spraying potential of a carbonated beverage.

PROBLEM/PURPOSE

How does temperature affect the amount of carbon dioxide in a carbonated beverage?

EXPERIMENT SUMMARY

You'll release the carbon dioxide from carbonated beverages and figure out how much gas is dissolved.

WHAT YOU NEED

▶ **6 cold 16- or 20- ounce (480 or 600 mL) carbonated beverages* in plastic bottles**

▶ **Scale that measures to 0.1 grams**

▶ **6 warm 16- or 20- ounce (480 or 600 mL) carbonated beverages* in plastic bottles**

*All of the bottles need to have the same amount of carbonated beverage.

EXPERIMENTAL PROCEDURE

1. Place the first cold unopened carbonated beverage on the scale, and record its initial mass. You will use this measurement to figure out how much mass was lost after you released the carbon dioxide.

2. Give the bottle 10 vigorous shakes. You should see bubbles building up in the bottle.

3. Very slowly and carefully loosen the cap of the bottle so that the gas escapes but not the carbonated beverage. You'll hear a hissing sound when the cap is loose enough. If you loosen the cap too much, carbonated beverage will spray out and you'll have to start over with a new bottle.

4. Place the bottle on the scale again and record the new mass. How much mass was lost when you let out the carbon dioxide?

5. Tighten the cap, and repeat steps 2 through 4 until the mass of the beverage no longer changes. Record the measurement each time.

6. Repeat the experiment with the rest of the cold beverages. Then repeat, using the warm carbonated beverages.

CONCLUSION

Make a line graph showing the amount of mass lost per shake. How much of the carbonated beverage was carbon dioxide? How many shakes did it take to release all of the gas? Which contained more gas, the warm or cold carbonated beverage?

TAKE A CLOSER LOOK

● The carbonated beverage in your bottle is under a pressure twice that of the atmosphere. If all of the carbon dioxide in it were released, it would fill about four carbonated beverage bottles.

● Glass bottles are better containers for carbonated drinks than plastic bottles. Carbon dioxide and air can diffuse through the plastic, and after a while your carbonated beverage will lose its fizz.

● The addition of carbon dioxide makes carbonated beverages slightly acidic and tastier. It also acts as a preservative so the carbonated beverage lasts longer.

WHAT ELSE YOU CAN DO

● Does diet carbonated beverage have a different amount of carbon dioxide than regular carbonated beverage?

Citrus Chemistry

In the 1700s, sailors discovered that drinking lime juice kept them from getting scurvy— a horrible disease where your gums bleed, your teeth fall out, and you get really weak and eventually die. The vitamin C kept their teeth and bones strong and helped their body produce red blood cells. How long does the vitamin C in juice last?

PROBLEM/PURPOSE

How does oxygen affect the amount of vitamin C in orange juice?

EXPERIMENT SUMMARY

You'll pour orange juice into cups, leave them uncovered in the refrigerator, and then test the juice every day to see how long the vitamin C lasts.

WHAT YOU NEED

- ▶ Measuring cup
- ▶ Water
- ▶ Metal pot
- ▶ Use of a stovetop
- ▶ Teaspoon
- ▶ Cornstarch
- ▶ Spoon for stirring
- ▶ Clear plastic cups
- ▶ Permanent marker
- ▶ Measuring spoons
- ▶ Iodine
- ▶ Eye dropper
- ▶ Orange juice
- ▶ Plastic wrap
- ▶ Refrigerator

EXPERIMENTAL PROCEDURE

1. Heat 1 cup (240 mL) of water until it boils. Slowly add 1 teaspoon (5 g) of cornstarch, and stir until it dissolves. When it cools, pour it into a cup and label it "starch solution" with the permanent marker.

2. Measure ½ teaspoon (2.5 mL) of the starch solution, and pour it into a new cup.

3. Add one or two drops of iodine to the starch solution until it turns blue.

4. Test the beginning amount of vitamin C in the orange juice. Use the eye dropper to add one drop of orange juice at a time to the cup. Count how many drops it takes until the blue color disappears. Record the number of drops on your data table. This measures the concentration of vitamin C in the orange juice. Discard the cup and its contents. Cover and store the starch solution in the refrigerator.

5. Label 10 new cups with the marker. Label half of them "uncovered" and the other half "covered."

6. Use the measuring cup to pour the same amount of orange juice into each cup. Cover the tops of the cups labeled "covered" with the plastic wrap. Put all the cups in the refrigerator.

7. Leave the cups undisturbed for 24 hours.

8. After 24 hours, prepare 10 new testing cups by putting ½ teaspoon (2.5 mL) of the starch solution into each cup. Then, add 1 to 2 drops of iodine until the solution in each turns blue.

9. Use the eye dropper to slowly add one drop of the first cup of uncovered orange juice to the first testing cup. Add one drop at a time until the blue color disappears. Record the number of drops you used in your data table. Repeat with the rest of the uncovered cups. Average your results.

10. Repeat step 9 with the rest of the covered cups. Average your results.

11. Re-cover the covered cups. Put all of the cups back in the refrigerator. Leave them undisturbed for another 24 hours, then repeat steps 8 through 10.

12. Continue this experiment every day until at least one of the cups has no more vitamin C in it. (You'll know, because no matter how much orange juice you add to the iodine solution, it will stay blue.) Make sure you record data for each day you are testing.

CONCLUSION

The strength of vitamin C in the orange juice is measured by the number of drops of orange juice needed to make the color of the iodine solution change. Which cup of orange juice contained more vitamin C after 24 hours? How long did it take to notice a decrease in vitamin C levels in both cups? How long did it take to eliminate the vitamin C from either cup of juice? Graph your results using a line graph. Then, make a recommendation for the storage of orange juice based on your findings.

TAKE A CLOSER LOOK

● In your experiment, the iodine reacts with the starch to produce a blue-black color. When the juice is added, the vitamin C and the iodine react to each other chemically. Because the iodine is reacting with the vitamin C, it no longer reacts with the starch, and the color disappears.

● The vitamin C in orange juice will *oxidize*, that is, combine with the oxygen in the air over time.

● Plants make vitamin C during photosynthesis. The more light a plant gets, the more vitamin C it produces. Vitamin C is *water-soluble*, which means it dissolves in water. It is also sensitive to heat, light, and exposure to air.

WHAT ELSE YOU CAN DO

● Compare how the strength of vitamin C declines over time when the juice is stored in different types of containers.

● Which part of the orange has the highest level of vitamin C, the peel, the pulp, or the juice?

The Bubble Olympics

The longest-lasting bubble stuck around for 341 days. That's a pretty strong bubble—how do you make a super bubble solution?

PROBLEM/PURPOSE

How does adding glycerin to a bubble solution affect the kind of bubbles it makes?

EXPERIMENT SUMMARY

You'll mix up several different bubble solutions, varying the amount of glycerin in each one. Then you'll use a fan to blow bubbles with the solutions.

WHAT YOU NEED

- ▶ **5 bowls**
- ▶ **Tape**
- ▶ **Permanent marker**
- ▶ **Measuring cup**
- ▶ **Water**
- ▶ **Liquid dish soap**
- ▶ **Spoon**
- ▶ **Liquid glycerin***
- ▶ **Measuring spoons**
- ▶ **Fan**
- ▶ **Bubble blower (see page 103)**
- ▶ **Measuring tape**
- ▶ **Helper**
- ▶ **Stopwatch**

You can find liquid glycerin at pharmacies.

EXPERIMENTAL PROCEDURE

1. Label each of the bowls 1 through 5 with the tape and the permanent marker.

2. Measure ¾ cup (180 mL) of cold water into bowl 1. Add ¼ cup (60 mL) of the liquid dish soap. Slowly stir the mixture together with the spoon. Try not to get too many bubbles in it.

3. Repeat step 2 in bowl 2, but also add ½ tablespoon (7.5 mL) of the liquid glycerin.

4. Repeat step 2 in bowl 3, but add 1 tablespoon (15 mL) of the liquid glycerin.

5. Repeat step 2 in bowl 4, but add 1½ tablespoons (22.5 mL) of the liquid glycerin.

6. Repeat step 2 in bowl 5, but add 2 tablespoons (30 mL) of the liquid glycerin.

7. Set up the fan in a wind-free location. Make sure you perform this part of the experiment somewhere that can get covered in soap bubbles.

8. For the next few steps, you're going to need a helper to measure the bubbles and run the stopwatch. Dip the bubble blower into the first bowl of bubble solution.

9. Start the stopwatch, and hold the bubble blower in front of the fan. Time how long the bubble expands, while your helper stands next to you with the measuring tape and measures the size of the bubble before it pops. Record these results.

10. Repeat steps 8 and 9 at least 10 times with the first solution. Then repeat the steps the same number of times with each solution. Make sure to blow all of your bubbles on the same day, as humidity can influence the size of the bubbles. Record your observations.

CONCLUSION

Which bubbles held the most air? Which ones were the biggest? Which ones lasted longest? Were there any other differences in the bubbles?

TAKE A CLOSER LOOK

● Soap molecules are *amphiphilic*, which means that one end of the molecule is *hydrophilic* (it loves being in water) and one end is *hydrophobic* (it repels water). The soap molecules form a border on either side of a layer of water, with their hydrophilic ends stuck in the water and their hydrophobic tails sticking out in either direction. The greasy end of the soap molecule (phobic end) keeps the water from evaporating off the surface of the bubble. This keeps the bubble around for longer.

● Bubbles are round because that's the shape that can hold the most volume with the least amount of surface area.

● Surface tension is the force that keeps water molecules together. Pure water will create bubbles, but the surface tension of the surrounding water is so great, the bubbles pop immediately. When you add soap, the surface tension of the water decreases enough to blow bubbles.

WHAT ELSE YOU CAN DO

● See if your bubble solutions get better if you let them sit for a certain amount of time.

● Experiment with the different colors in the soap film. What colors are present? Can you predict when the bubble will pop based on the colors in it?

Making a Bubble Blower

WHAT YOU NEED

▶ **Wire**
▶ **Wire cutters**
▶ **Cylindrical object (a cup or container)**

WHAT YOU DO

1. Cut a length of the wire with the wire cutters.

2. Bend one end of the wire around the cylindrical object to create a loop.

3. Twist the end around the stem of the wire to hold the loop in place.

4. Before you use your bubble blower, get it wet. This will help you blow better bubbles.

Take a Closer Look
You've Got Glycerin in You!

Glycerin is a thick, colorless, slightly sweet liquid that's found in animal and vegetable fats. It has all sorts of uses besides just making bubbles. Glycerin is used to make dynamite and lubricate hydraulic jacks. It's also put into lotions, cosmetics, toothpaste, and ink. You even eat a lot of glycerin. It's used as a sugar substitute in many foods, to can fruit (like jams and jellies), to keep the sugar in candy from crystallizing, and to hold the air in ice cream.

Food or Fuel?

Adult Supervision Required

The first thing most people look at when they're buying food is how many Calories the food contains. A *Calorie* is a unit of energy. (Specifically, it's the amount of energy it takes to raise the temperature of one kilogram of water by one degree Celsius.)

PROBLEM/PURPOSE

How much energy do foods contain?

EXPERIMENT SUMMARY

You'll burn a variety of foods and measure the amount of heat given off to determine the Calories contained in each type of food.

WHAT YOU NEED

▶ Calorimeter can (see page 105)
▶ Measuring cup
▶ Scale*
▶ 50 mL cold water
▶ Ring stand (also known as a lab stand)*
▶ Clamp*
▶ Brazil nut
▶ Thermometer
▶ Safety lighter
▶ Stopwatch
▶ Marshmallow
▶ Cheese puff and other food items
▶ Adult helper

Ask your science teacher if you can borrow one.

EXPERIMENTAL PROCEDURE

1. All of the measurements in this experiment should be done with the metric system. This will make your calculations much, much easier and more accurate, so remember to record your measurements in milliliters, grams, and Celsius throughout this project.

2. Make a calorimeter can (see page 105). Record the mass of the empty calorimeter can.

3. Add 50 mL of cold water to the calorimeter can, and record its mass again.

4. Place the calorimeter can in the ring on the ring stand. Use the dowel to suspend the can from the ring.

5. Place the clamp under the calorimeter can. Adjust the ring stand so that the bottom of the can is about 1 inch (2.5 cm) above the clamp (see project photo).

6. Record the mass of the brazil nut, and place the nut in the clamp.

7. Place the thermometer in the calorimeter can and record the initial temperature of the water in Celsius. Remove the thermometer.

8. Position the brazil nut under the center of the calorimeter can. Use the safety lighter to light it. Start the stopwatch. If the brazil nut stops burning while you're performing this part of the experiment, quickly re-light it.

9. Slowly stir the water with the thermometer while the brazil nut burns. Be careful not to touch the bottom or sides of the can with the thermometer. (This may alter your results.)

10. When the brazil nut is completely burnt, stop the stopwatch. Record the final temperature of the water, and the amount of time it took the nut to burn.

11. Measure and record the mass of what is left of the brazil nut.

12. Clean off the stand, and empty the water out of the calorimeter can. Repeat steps 3 through 12 for each of the other food samples.

CONCLUSION

Calculate the energy in Calories that each food sample contained. To do this, first you will need to figure out energy gained by the water and the change in mass that the food sample underwent.

To find the energy gained (in Calories) by the water, you will need to use this equation:

Energy gained by water = (mass of water in mL) x (change in temperature of water in °C) x 998 Calories/g °C

1. To calculate the mass of the water, subtract the mass of the calorimeter can (step 2) from the combined mass of the can and water (step 3).

2. To calculate the change in temperature of the water, subtract its initial temperature (step 7) from its final temperature (step 10).

To calculate the change in mass of a food sample, subtract the initial mass (step 6) from the final mass (step 11).

Find the energy in Calories contained in each food sample by taking the energy gained by the water and dividing it by the change in mass of the food in grams. Do this for each food sample you burned. Get an adult to help you with these equations.

Which food heated the water the most? Which of the foods had the greatest energy content? Which of the foods is the best energy source? How did your results compare to the food manufacturer's Calorie count?

TAKE A CLOSER LOOK

● The Sun is the original source of energy for all of our foods, especially those from plants. Plants can transform the radiant energy into chemical energy. This energy is used to make substances such as fats, carbohydrates, and other high-energy chemicals. When these chemicals are broken down in our bodies (or burned), they release energy.

WHAT ELSE YOU CAN DO

● How do the energy content values you measured compare to the value listed in dietary books?

● Determine the energy contents of different types of nuts, such as peanuts, walnuts, pecans or almonds.

● Explore other combustible foods such as lima beans, kidney beans, pine nuts, lard, and dry coconut.

Making a Calorimeter Can

WHAT YOU NEED

▶ **Metal can**
▶ **Adult helper**
▶ **Drill**
▶ **Dowel**

INSTRUCTIONS

1. Remove all the paper labels from the can, and wash it out well.

2. Have an adult help you drill or poke two holes in the can just below the top rim. The holes should be large enough for the dowel to fit through easily.

"Fall"ty Predictions

Every year, the leaves on the trees start out green (with a few exceptions) and end up a riot of colors in the fall. How do the leaves go from plain green to red, orange, and yellow?

PROBLEM/PURPOSE

How do the types of pigments in a green leaf determine its fall color?

EXPERIMENT SUMMARY

You'll perform an experiment early in the year to see what color pigments green leaves contain. In the fall, you'll compare the colors of the same kinds of leaves to see if you can predict what color a green leaf is going to turn.

WHAT YOU NEED

- ▶ One green leaf from any 3 of the following trees: sycamore, black cherry, sugar maple, birch, red maple, ash, black gum, and red oak
- ▶ Field guide to trees
- ▶ Coffee filter
- ▶ Scissors
- ▶ 3 small glasses
- ▶ Tape
- ▶ 3 pencils
- ▶ Coin
- ▶ Ruler
- ▶ Isopropyl alcohol (rubbing alcohol)
- ▶ One fall-colored leaf from each of the same trees

EXPERIMENTAL PROCEDURE

1. Collect one green leaf from at least three different trees. Use a tree field guide to help you identify what kind of tree it is. Put a leaf from each tree in the appropriate page of the book to keep track of which leaf is which.

2. Cut the coffee filter into 1-inch-wide (2.5 cm) strips, and label each glass with a piece of tape, identifying which leaf you're testing.

3. Wrap the end of one of the coffee filter strips around a pencil. Tape it in place so that when the pencil rests across the top of the glass, the strip will hang into the glass. It should not touch the sides or the bottom.

4. Put the filter strip on a flat, hard surface. Place the first leaf on top of the filter strip, near the bottom. Use the coin to rub back and forth over the leaf until you have a horizontal line of pigment on the filter strip, approximately 1 inch (2.5 cm) from the end of the strip.

5. Pour a small amount of alcohol into the glass, just filling the bottom. (Keep your filter strip well out of the way when you do this!)

6. Place the pencil with the filter strip across the glass so that the bottom of the strip touches the alcohol but the pigment line does not. You may need to adjust the amount of alcohol in the glass. Take the filter strip out of the glass before you do this. Splashing alcohol directly on the pigment will mess up the experiment, so be careful.

7. Wait 25 to 30 minutes, or until alcohol spreads up the filter through the pigment and reaches the pencil. Record your observations.

8. Repeat steps 2 through 7 for each leaf.

9. Repeat the entire experiment once the trees have changed to their fall color. Compare your results to the green leaves.

CONCLUSION

What pigments did you observe in the strips from the green leaves? How were these different from the pigments in the strips from the same tree in the fall? Could you predict the color of a particular leaf based on the pigment you observed from the green leaf? Why or why not?

TAKE A CLOSER LOOK

● The pigments found in leaves are involved in making food for the plant: a process called *photosynthesis*. Different pigments absorb different wavelengths of light to make this process more efficient for the plant. Some of the pigments you may see are *Chlorophyll A* and *Chlorophyll B*. These are the major photosynthetic pigments and are responsible for the green color of

the leaf. Other pigments you may see are *carotenes* (orange), *xanthophylls* (yellow), and *anthocyanins* (red). The green chlorophylls hide the other pigments of the leaves. With this experiment, you can separate the pigments that are hidden by the chlorophyll into bands of color.

Fall color of common trees:

Sycamore: yellow
Black gum: red-orange
Black cherry: yellow
Red maple: red, orange
Ash: yellow
Red oaks: red
Sugar maple: yellow, orange, red
Birch: yellow
White oaks: brown to red

Now That's Repelling!

There are tons of things in life we like to keep dry. One of the ways to protect our shoes, rugs, couches, and clothing is to spray them with water repellent.

PROBLEM/PURPOSE

Which brand of spray-on water repellent does the best job?

EXPERIMENT SUMMARY

You'll test several different brands of spray-on water repellent by spraying them onto fabric. Then, you'll pour water over the fabric and see which one keeps the water out best.

WHAT YOU NEED

▶ **Fabric**
▶ **Scissors**
▶ **2 clear measuring cups**
▶ **Rubber bands**
▶ **Several brands of spray-on water repellent**
▶ **Water**

EXPERIMENTAL PROCEDURE

1. Cut out a piece of fabric with the scissors. It should be big enough to fit over the mouth of the measuring cup with enough overlap for the rubber band to hold it in place.

2. Use the piece of fabric you cut in step 1 to cut one piece of fabric for each type of spray-on repellent you have. You should also have one additional piece of fabric.

3. Secure one piece of fabric over the mouth of the measuring cup with a rubber band.

4. Spray a different type of spray-on repellent onto each of the remaining pieces of fabric.

5. Label the fabric on the edge that will overlap the mouth of the measuring cup so that you know which repellent is where. Let the repellents dry.

6. While the repellent dries, slowly and carefully pour ½ cup (120 mL) of water onto the piece of fabric you put over the measuring cup in step 3. Don't let any spill, and stop pouring if the fabric can no longer hold any water. Wait 5 minutes.

7. Measure the amount of water in the measuring cup. Record your results. Pour the water out of the measuring cup, and dry it out.

8. When the repellent has set, use the rubber band to secure one of those pieces of fabric to the measuring cup. Repeat steps 6 and 7. Do this for each piece of fabric.

CONCLUSION

Which fabric piece let the most water through? Which one let the least amount of water through? Did one repellent have a longer drying time than the others? How would this affect your experiment? Make a bar graph to show your results.

TAKE A CLOSER LOOK

● Water repellent forms a smooth coating over the tiny holes in fabric. The coating is so smooth that the gaps in it are smaller than water molecules. Because the water molecules can't pass through the protective coating, they stay on the surface where they can be easily wiped away.

● Stains form when a solution of water and something colored (like grape juice) is spilled on some sort of fiber. The water helps the solution soak in, then the water evaporates and the colored stuff sticks to the fibers.

Templates for Parachute Power (page 58)

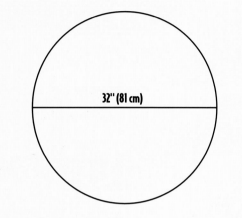

32" (81 cm)

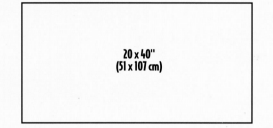

20 x 40"
(51 x 107 cm)

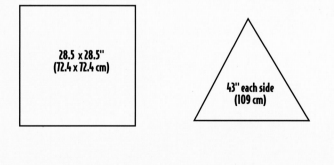

28.5 x 28.5"
(72.4 x 72.4 cm)

43" each side
(109 cm)

Acknowledgments

It takes a metropolis to put a book like this together, and there are tons of people we'd like to thank. So, here it goes. We'd like to thank:

- Hope Buttita, for her wonderful projects

- Elizabeth Snoke, for providing projects and being our technical consultant

- Orrin Lundgren, for once again coming through with wonderful illustrations

- Celia Naranjo, for creating a beautiful book

- Steve Mann, for taking the pretty pictures

- Jessy Mauney and Shannon Yokeley, for their production assistance

- Megan Kirby, for dressing up and hamming it up

- Nathalie Mornu, for her thorough editorial help

- Robert D. Miller, for letting us use his photographs

- Duncan Rice, Stacey Budge, Deborah Morgenthal, Carol Taylor, Sunita Patterson, Veronika Gunter, Nicole Tuggle, and everyone else at Lark Books, for their support, friendship, and assistance

- Anna, Camille, Candace, Jasmine, Lacey, Marcus, Megan (mummy mom!), Noah, Rabb Scott, Sam, Sarah, and Tye, for being fantastic models

- Jinx Pace, for changing the oil

- Obidiah and Jax , for sticking out their tongues when asked (woof!)

Photography Credits

Brand X Pictures: Bugs (pages 26-27), Dogs (page 36), Compost (page 51), and Bunch of Balloons (page 98)

Comstock: Fortune Teller (page 31) and Compost (page 51)

© Corbis: Can of Worms (page 50), Parachute (page 59), Sandy Feet (page 63), Crowd at the Beach (page 64), Suntan Lotion (page 79), and Carlsbad Caverns (page 81)

Library of Congress: school photos (pages 23, 56, and 85)

© Chris Lisle/CORBIS: Head of Tollund Man (page 90)

Robert D. Miller: Night photos (page 73)

Photodisc: Mars (page 12)

Seattle Support Group: Autumn Leaves (page 107)

USDA: Mosquito (page 26)

Index

A Note About Suppliers

Usually, the supplies you need for making the projects in Lark books can be found at your local craft supply store, discount mart, home improvement center, or retail shop relevant to the topic of the book. Occasionally, however, you may need to buy materials or tools from specialty suppliers. In order to provide you with the most up-to-date information, we have created a listing of suppliers on our Web site, which we update on a regular basis. Visit us at www.larkbooks.com, click on "Craft Supply Sources," and then click on the relevant topic. You will find numerous companies listed with their web address and/or mailing address and phone number.

Hey Kids!

Got a cool science experiment you'd like to share with us? Got a great book idea? We want to hear all about it. Send us an e-mail at kids@larkbooks.com, or send us some snail mail at Kids at Lark, Lark Books, 67 Broadway, Asheville, NC, 28801.